The Theory of Transaction in Institutional Economics

T0311500

Despite abundant literature on transaction costs, there is little comprehensive analysis available regarding what the transaction is or how it works. Drawing on both Old and New Institutional Economics, and on a variety of interdisciplinary sources, this monograph traces the history of the meaning of transaction in institutional economics, mapping its topicality and use over time.

This manuscript treats the idea of transaction as a construct with legal, competitive and political dimensions and connects different approaches within institutional economics. The book covers the contributions of key thinkers from different schools, including Ronald H. Coase, John R. Commons, Robert Lee Hale, Oliver Hart, Mancur Olson, Thorstein Veblen and Oliver E. Williamson.

This book will be of interest to advanced students and researchers of institutional economics, law and economics, and the history of economic thought.

Massimiliano Vatiero (Ph.D., University of Siena) is an Assistant Professor of Political Economy at the Department of Economics and Management (DEM) of the University of Trento (Italy), and "Brenno Galli" Chair of Law and Economics at the Law Institute (IDUSI) of the Università della Svizzera italiana.

Routledge Studies in the History of Economics

Macroeconomics without the Errors of Keynes
The Quantity Theory of Money, Saving, and Policy
James C.W. Ahiakpor

The Political Economy of the Han Dynasty and Its Legacy
Edited by Cheng Lin, Terry Peach and Wang Fang

A History of Utilitarian Ethics
Samuel Hollander

The Economic Thought of Michael Polanyi
Gábor Biró

Ideas in the History of Economic Development
The Case of Peripheral Countries
Edited by Estrella Trincado, Andrés Lazzarini and Denis Melnik

Ordoliberalism and European Economic Policy
Between Realpolitik and Economic Utopia
Edited by Malte Dold and Tim Krieger

The Economic Thought of Sir James Steuart
First Economist of the Scottish Enlightenment
Edited by José M. Menudo

A History of Feminist and Gender Economics
Giandomenica Becchio

The Theory of Transaction in Institutional Economics
A History
Massimiliano Vatiero

For more information about this series, please visit www.routledge.com/series/SE0341

The Theory of Transaction in Institutional Economics

A History

Massimiliano Vatiero

Routledge
Taylor & Francis Group

LONDON AND NEW YORK

First published 2021
by Routledge
2 Park Square, Milton Park, Abingdon, Oxon OX14 4RN

and by Routledge
52 Vanderbilt Avenue, New York, NY 10017

Routledge is an imprint of the Taylor & Francis Group, an informa business

© 2021 Massimiliano Vatiero

The right of Massimiliano Vatiero to be identified as author of this work has been asserted by him in accordance with sections 77 and 78 of the Copyright, Designs and Patents Act 1988.

British Library Cataloguing-in-Publication Data
A catalogue record for this book is available from the British Library

Library of Congress Cataloging-in-Publication Data
A catalog record for this book has been requested

ISBN: 978-0-367-19469-7 (hbk)
ISBN: **978-0-367-53030-3 (pbk)**
ISBN: 978-0-429-20261-2 (ebk)

Typeset in Bembo
by Apex CoVantage, LLC

To My Mum

Contents

Preface

[H]istory records more frequent and more spectacular instances of the triumph of imbecile institutions over life and culture than of people who have by force of instinctive insight saved themselves alive out of a desperately precarious institutional solution.

Veblen (1914:25)

Writing a book can be a rather lonely endeavour. Luckily, many people have accompanied me on my "long journey" to prepare this manuscript.

The journey commenced 15 or more years ago at the University of Siena, under my stimulating teachers. After, it was carried out at the Università della Svizzera italiana and completed at the University of Trento. I have learned a ton from these years as traveller.

The project benefitted greatly from conversations with colleagues from many institutions. First and above all, Ugo Pagano of the University of Siena, for a great number of helpful discussions on all aspects of the book's topics. I am also grateful to Luca Fiorito of the University of Palermo and Nicola Giocoli of the University of Pisa for guiding me on the historical aspects of my research; Antonio Nicita of the University of Rome "La Sapienza" for helping me to understand the antitrust and contractual consequences of a broader idea of transaction; and Mark Roe of the Harvard Law School for encouraging me to develop the political economy of institutions.

I also received exceptionally helpful comments on this manuscript from Giuseppe Bellantuono (University of Trento), Filippo Belloc (University of Siena), Luigi Bonatti (University of Trento), David Gindis (University of Hertfordshire), Nicola Meccheri (University of Pisa), Uriel Procaccia (Tel-Aviv University), Anna Tzanaki (European University Institute) and Paola Villa (University of Trento).

I express great gratitude to Oliver Hart for our conversations on various parts of the book at Harvard University and various conferences.

Over the years, I have had the chance to present early versions of parts of the book at seminars at the Bucerius Law School of Hamburg, the Bilkent

University of Ankara, the University of Pisa, the University of Siena and the University of Trento; at various academic conferences of the World Interdisciplinary Network for Institutional Research (WINIR), the Society for Institutional and Organizational Economics (SIOE, former ISNIE), the European Association of Law and Economics (EALE), the Italian Society of Law and Economics (SIDE), the Italian Association for the History of Economics (STOREP) and the Italian Society of Economists (SIE); and at the Siena-Toronto-Tel Aviv workshop of Law and Economics (STILE) and MetaLawEcon workshop. The comments and feedback I received at these venues helped to clarify my arguments.

Moreover, I wrote significant parts of the book while visiting a number of institutions. In particular, I gratefully acknowledge financial support provided by a Visiting Fellowship from the Comparative Corporate Governance and Finance Program at Harvard Law School. This book benefitted also from a grant from the Italian Association for the History of Economics (STOREP).

In writing this book, I enjoyed plentiful financial support from the "Brenno Galli" Fund at the Università della Svizzera italiana and generous aid from Galli's family at Lugano. I also thank all members of the Law Institute (IDUSI) at the Università della Svizzera italiana for their important support of the entire project and for helping me accommodate periods of writing in the life of our institute.

Finally, I am grateful to the editorial team at Routledge for the care they have given to this project over the last two years. I also thank anonymous referees for their constructive comments on the original book project and the first version of the manuscript.

Of course, none of the abovementioned friends, colleagues or institutions is responsible for any flaws in my work on the concept of transaction.

Lugano (Switzerland)/Trento (Italy), October 2019
MV

The roadmap

The transaction is the basic unit of analysis of institutionalism. The aim of this volume is to provide a historical conceptualization of the transaction.

A *trans-action* represents a complex *act* in a composite institutional setting that *trans*-fers control over a resource. A transaction involves not only the actions of two actual *trans-actors* but also the actions expected by potential transactors (e.g., alternatives to two actual transactors) and the power of the public official actor. This idea of transaction, originally formulated by John Commons (and that for Oliver Williamson represents the unit of transaction cost economics), is able to take into account and combine different facets of transactions and transactor's choices.

This book develops the three main dimensions which shape *each* transaction: the legal, competitive and political dimensions. The legal and political dimensions concern the relationships between each transactor and the public official actor. The legal dimension, in particular, involves the effects of rule-making and rule-enforcing processes over a transactor's choices, whereas the political dimension involves the influence of each transactor over polity. Finally, the competitive dimension concerns the impact of the market (especially throughout price) on a transactor's choices and – vice versa – how a transactor's choices affect market configuration and prices.

The book is divided into six chapters. Chapter 1 maps the meanings of transaction and their uses over time. It deals with the four most important (in my opinion!) authors of transactional theory: Ronald Coase, John Commons, Robert Lee Hale and Oliver Williamson. Chapter 2 introduces the narrative of the book: each transaction comprises three dimensions: the legal, competitive and political dimensions. Chapter 3 focuses on the legal dimension of a transaction and, in particular, shows that, given the adversarial nature of legal positions, the definition of rights may generate positional goods concerns. Chapter 4 involves transactions with specific investments and sheds light on the role of the outside market in both the emergence of the holdup problem and its remedies. This chapter also develops a "trade-off" between institutional remedies à la Oliver Hart and à la Oliver Williamson. Chapter 5 considers the fact that rules are not exogenous and immutable but rather that people can affect them via polity. This chapter centres on transactions within firms and their relationships with political arena. Finally, Chapter 6 summarizes the book's major findings and implications and identifies one (just one, but remarkable) avenue for future research.

1 Mapping the meaning of "transaction"

The transaction is the basic unit of analysis of institutionalism. Although the definition of institutionalism is complex and quite partial, this book refers to theories which hold that "(i) institutions[1] do matter, [and that] (ii) the determinants of institutions are susceptible to analysis" (Matthews 1986:903). The "Old Institutionalism" of John Commons and Thorstein Veblen (in rigorous alphabetical order) and the New Institutional Economics of Ronald Coase and the *Coasians* such as Oliver Hart, Douglass North, Mancur Olson and Oliver Williamson (again, in rigorous alphabetical order) constitute key streams, even if different and sometimes in contradiction, of institutionalism (cf. also DiMaggio and Powell 1991; Williamson 1996a; Rutherford 2001).

The main focuses of the institutionalism programme are transactions and their costs, or transaction costs. After Coase's (1960) article (and in particular after Stigler's formulation of the Coase theorem in 1966), there was an exponential increase in the use of word "transaction" in academic works, as Figure 1.1 suggests.[2] This explains why Ronald Coase and his 1960 article are supposed to be the starting point of the theory of transaction costs. For this reason, this chapter starts from the idea(s) of transaction as described in Coase (especially Coase 1937, 1960).

Even if the *theory of transaction costs* does originate with the contributions of Ronald Coase, the *theory of transaction* is from earlier. Indeed, the first comprehensive formulation of an idea of transaction in the social sciences was conceived by John Commons in the beginning of the 1920s, as representing a unit of analysis of capitalism and its peculiarities.[3] Williamson's praise of John Commons as the great forerunner of transaction cost economics is well known among interpreters of institutionalist thought and methodology, especially as his tribute particularly concerns Commons's idea of transaction as the basic unit of transaction cost economics (e.g., Williamson 1981:549–550, 1985a:3, 6, 1985b:179, 1988:571, 1996b:50, 1996c:152, 1999:5, 2000:599). However, both Williamson himself and other transaction cost economists have poorly applied Commons's proper idea of transaction.

Documents by year

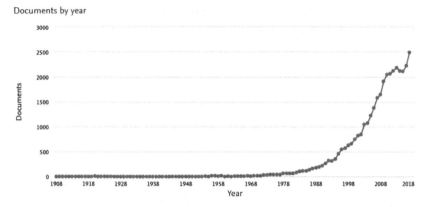

Figure 1.1 The term "transaction" in the title, abstract and keywords of academic publications.

Source: Scopus's documents, including, articles, books, chapters in books, etc., limited to three subject areas: business, management and accounting; economics, econometrics and finance; and social science; 1908–2018.

1.1.   The ideas of transaction in Coase (1937) and (1960)

Ronald Coase was awarded the Sveriges Riksbank Prize in Economic Sciences in Memory of Alfred Nobel in 1991 (at the age of 81) for two main articles: "The nature of the firm," published when he was 27, and "The problem of social cost," which appeared more than 20 years later.

Although they are clearly linked thematically – both investigate the costs of transactions – the two articles are the consequence of different contextual and historical environments. In the 1937 article, Coase aims to challenge the laissez-faire ideology of time on the basis of the postulation that "the market system works itself." In the article of 1960, instead, arguing that under certain conditions the market transaction can efficiently substitute state-directed transaction, he has a different scope: to question the claim that state intervention in the economy is necessary or desirable, as economic thought and political debate of the 1950s advised. The conceptualization of transaction in Ronald Coase's thought shows a clear example of the influence of the historical context and political debate on the history of economic thought. A similar account holds for the formulation and use of the concept of the transaction in works by John Commons, Oliver Williamson and other scholars.[4]

More in detail, in 1937, Coase asked why the firm emerges and replied that the reason is that there are costs in using the price mechanism. Moreover, he adds that these costs can be saved by the use of an alternative, hierarchical structure such as the firm:[5] "[T]he operation of a market costs something and by forming an organization and allowing some authority (an 'entrepreneur') to direct the resources, certain marketing costs are saved" (Coase 1937:392). In doing so, Coase considers *market transaction* and *transaction within the firm* as alternative modes for organizing the *same* transaction. On the one hand, "price movements direct production, which is co-ordinated through a series of exchange transactions on the market" (Coase 1937:388); on the other hand, "[w]ithin a firm these market transactions are eliminated, and in place of the complicated market structure with exchange transactions is substituted the entrepreneur-co-ordinator, who directs production" (Coase 1937:388).

In Coase's (1937) article, "transaction" (singular or plural form) is mentioned 54 times and about one in every three refers to transactions within the firm. Table 1.1 reports expressions (in italics) and pages referring to "transaction" in Coase (1937). Note that there could be many expressions on each page; for instance, on page 396 of the article in 1937, the term "transaction" is repeated 15 times, ten of which refer to market transactions and five to transactions within a firm.

Interestingly, in Coase (1960), "transaction" (singular or plural form) is quoted (solely) 28 times, but he refers to transaction(s) within a firm only in two cases (see Table 1.2).

Table 1.1 Expressing transactions in Coase (1937).

Transaction(s)	*Words*
• in the market	• *exchange transaction(s)* (Coase 1937:388, 391, 393, 394, 395, 396, 397, 402, 403, 404)
	• *market transaction(s)* (Coase 1937:388, 392, 393, 394, 395, 396)
	• *transaction(s) in the open market* (Coase 1937:394, 396)
	• *marketing transaction(s)* (Coase 1937:395, 399)
• within the firm	• *transaction(s) organized within a firm* (Coase 1937:393, 394, 395, 396)
	• *transaction(s) organized (by the entrepreneur)* (Coase 1937:393, 394, 395, 396, 397)
	• *organized transaction(s)* (Coase 1937:393, 396)

Table 1.2 Expressing transactions in Coase (1960).

Referring to transaction(s)	*Words*
• in the market	• *market transaction(s)* (Coase 1960:5, 6, 8, 10, 13, 15, 16, 17, 18, 19, 37)
	• *transaction on the market* (Coase 1960:17)
• within the firm	• *transaction through a firm* (Coase 1960:16)
	• *transactions within the firm* (Coase 1960:17)

In Coase (1960), the idea of market transaction stands for a transfer, recombination or rearrangement of legal rights. Using Coase's words, "if such market transactions are costless, such a *rearrangement of rights* will always take place if it would lead to an increase in the value of production" (Coase 1960:15, italics added); "[o]nce the costs of carrying out market transactions are taken into account it is clear that such a *rearrangement of rights* will only be undertaken when . . ." (Coase 1960:15, italics added); and "given that the costs of market transactions make a *rearrangement of rights* impossible" (Coase 1960:38, italics added). As Coase (1992:717, italics added) later specifies, "what are traded on the market are not, as is often supposed by economists, physical entities, but the *rights to perform certain actions.*"

In 1937, Coase identifies the key difference between a market transaction and a transaction within the firm. In a widely quoted passage referring to labour, Coase argues that workers move (or do not move) from department Y to department X not because the price of X has changed enough relative to the price of Y to make the move worthwhile for them but rather because they have been ordered to do so (cf. Coase 1937:387; see also Coase 1972:63). Namely, the transaction within a firm comes from an entrepreneur's orders. A market transaction thus represents a (re)allocation of legal entitlements over resources using the price mechanism, while a transaction within the firm is a (re)allocation which rests on hierarchy and administrative decisions (that are, nevertheless, legally permitted).

There is, however, a third type of transaction which is quite poorly expressed in Coase (1937, 1960): the transaction by regulation or by the state. The only implicit reference is in Coase (1960): "The government is, in a sense, a super-firm" (Coase 1960:17). For instance, a legislature that passes a law or a court that issues an edict that in some respect transfers economic resources from one agent to another via legal commands and coercion of the state represents a third type of transaction.

In sum, Coase identifies three types of transactions:

1   market transactions,
2   transactions within a firm, and
3   transactions within a super-firm (i.e., the state).

A market transaction is thus an action that transfers or rearranges property rights over economic resources via the price mechanism. A transaction within a firm represents, quite differently, a rearrangement of resources (typically of factors of production) by legally permitted orders. Finally, there is the transaction by the decisions and commands of the state. All these types of transactions are *legal* constructs in which there is an actual action of transferring, allocating and rearranging the rights over resources.

The general problem is to choose the appropriate institutional construct – this is the main message of Coase's contributions.

Finally, Coase notes that there is a link between transactions within the firm and those in the market. Coase writes, quoting Maurice Dobb on Adam Smith's conception of the capitalist, that

> [i]t began to be seen that there was something more important than the relations inside each factory or unit captained by an undertaker; there were the relations of the undertaker with the rest of the economic world *outside* his immediate sphere . . . the undertaker busies himself with the division of labour inside each firm and he plans and organises consciously [. . . but . . .] he is related to the much larger economic specialisation, of which he himself is merely one specialised unit. Here, he plays his part as a single cell in a larger organism, mainly unconscious of the wider role he fills.
>
> (Coase 1937:389, quoting Maurice Dobb, emphasis added)

In 1937, Coase thus suggests that the economic outcome is the result of the actions of agents within the firm *and* in the market. That is, the transaction within the firm is also related to the outside market. This insight will be developed here by using Commons's formulation of transaction.

1.2. John Commons's formulation of transaction

According to Commons, a transaction represents an institutional delivery of the control or ownership over a resource (cf. Commons 1924, 1931, 1932, 1934, 1959), which involves five actors (see especially Commons 1924). First, as for Coase, each transaction for Commons relies on a legal dimension. In the words of Commons, "[t]ransactions determine legal control, while the classical and hedonic economics was concerned with physical control" (Commons 1931:648); or

> [t]ransactions are the means, under operation of law and custom, of acquiring and alienating legal control of commodities, or legal control of the labor and management that will produce and deliver or exchange the commodities and services, forward to the ultimate consumers.
>
> (Commons 1931:656–657)

Second, each transaction is a delivery, transfer or rearrangement of rights over resources. Even this second characteristic fits with Coase's formulation of transaction. Lastly, and this is one of the main originalities of Commons's idea of transaction (with respect to Coase), each transaction concerns five actors. There are two actual transactors, who are engaged in the transaction, but there are also two potential transactors, one competitor (or counterparty) for each actual transactor. These two potential transactors are necessary to define the opportunity costs of transaction. Finally, there is a further, fifth actor, a public official actor, who guarantees a perfect fit between the entitlements of all transactors.

The transaction is therefore "not an individual seeking his own pleasure: it is five individuals doing something to each other within the limits of working rules laid down by those who determine how disputes shall be decided" (Commons 1924:69). Again, in 1934, he writes,

> These individual actions are really trans–actions – that is, actions between individuals – as well as individual behaviour. It is this shift from commodities, individuals, and exchanges to transactions and working rules of collective action that marks the transition from the classical and hedonic schools to the institutional schools of economic thinking. The shift is a change in the ultimate unit of economic investigation, from commodities and individuals to transactions between individuals.
>
> (Commons 1934:73)

In similar terms, "[t]hese individual actions are really *trans*-actions instead of either individual behavior or the 'exchange' of commodities" (Commons 1931:652, italics in the original).

For instance, consider an exchange between a seller, say Robinson (who is denoted by $R1$), and a buyer, say Friday (who is denoted by $F1$), as in Figure 1.2. According to Commons, the exchange between Robinson and Friday also depends on alternatives in the outside market: an "alternative Robinson" (indicated by $R2$) who competes with $R1$ and represents an alternative counterparty for transactor $F1$, and an "alternative Friday" (indicated with $F2$) who competes with $F1$ and represents an alternative

Figure 1.2 Five actors in Commons's transaction.

counterparty for transactor $R1$. Finally, there is a public official actor P who defines and enforces the rules of the transaction (see Figure 1.2). Commons's main idea is that there are never just two parties exchanging goods between themselves in a transaction; rather, there is also 'the market' given by a second potential buyer, a second potential seller; and, finally, there is a ruling authority to define rights and decide disputes.[6]

It is worth noting two aspects of this idea of transaction. The first is that in a transaction there is both a horizontal and a vertical characterization. The horizontal character relies on the free competition between two transactors at the same level of the supply-and-demand chain, e.g., the competition between $R1$ and $R2$. The vertical character of competition is instead between two transactors placed at different levels of the supply-and-demand chain, e.g., between $R1$ and $F1$. This second character, rather than the horizontal one, was the image of competition that classical economists primarily emphasized. For them, competition meant foremost the contrast of interests in an exchange (viz., contract), each trying to get the most from the bargain (Giocoli 2014, 2017).

Second, in his idea of transaction, Commons makes the role of the public official in transactions explicit. Again, classical economists had a quite similar position. For instance, in his "Lectures on Jurisprudence," Adam Smith explicated the importance of property rights and their enforcement: the "first and chief design of every system of government . . . is to give each one the secure and peaceable possession of his own property" (Smith 1762–1766 in 1978:5). Hence, Adam Smith believed that market required the support by appropriate legal structures and an effective administration of justice (Medema 2009:24). In Commons, the role of the public official actor is to stabilize expectations by allowing transactors to fairly predict the legal consequences of the specific actions of the transactors. In particular, the public official correlates the right of one transactor with duty (in the case of a legal claim for obtaining something) or with exposure (in the case of restraining someone from doing something) for another transactor. When a right ends, an exposure begins; when a duty ends, liberty begins. Because of jural correlatives (that will be developed in Chapter 3 using Wesley Newcomb Hohfeld's scheme), the public official confers uniformity on the transactors' expectations. In the words of Commons,

> the only procedure that will *correlate* the wishes and fears and prevent anarchy is to resort to a third person [i.e., a public official] of an earthly quality whom each consents to obey, or each is compelled to obey. Thus we reach the social necessity of judges, chiefs, kings, despots, priests, governors, managers, and so on, whose behavioristic function, guided more or less by ethical beliefs which they share with some of the others, is that of correlating in practice conflicting assertions and denials of

rights and duties. Individuals with opposite interests or beliefs cannot always agree on the correlation, but the correlation is necessary in order to hold together the constituents of a collective will . . . the correlation of rights and duties is not a conclusion of logic, as is often inferred, but is a command of government.

(Commons 1924:86–87, italics in original)

Moreover, Commons takes the role of transactors in the political arena seriously. The rights of one party are the interests which society protects via the public official actor when in conflict with other interests. As Commons writes, "the correlation of rights and duties is not a conclusion of logic, as is often inferred, but is a command of government" (Commons 1924:86–87). In other words, each institution emerges as a result of the conflicting interests of transactors. In doing so, Commons advances the idea that neither polity nor economy are given, independent and self-sufficient but rather that both emerge through a process of coevolution. Both capitalism and its legal foundations are outcomes of an ongoing interaction between interest groups competing and cooperating in a world of scarcity (Biddle and Samuels 2007). Thus, "the fabric of social relationships which grow up in a community or a society" (Commons 1934:74) moulds the transaction. Therefore, it could be a slight oversimplification to consider transaction à la Commons as a *microscope* on transactor's choices. It represents also a *telescope* to look at causes and consequences concerning wider domains, besides the simple relationship between two transactors.

Commons also distinguishes between "authorized" and "authoritative" transactions (Commons 1924). Authoritative transactions are hierarchical, while authorized transactions are not. This does not mean that authorized transactions do not ever involve legal power but simply that power is not "built" into the nature of the transaction (Commons 1924:107). The authoritative transaction differs from the authorized one wherein the former conceives the legal relationship between a private individual and a public official, while the latter conceives the relationship between private transactors. The most notable authorized transaction is the exchange, which Commons calls the bargaining transaction. The bargaining transaction derives from the familiar formula of a market, which, at the time of negotiation, consists of the actual buyer and actual seller and of the best potential two alternatives (the best alternative seller and the best alternative buyer), all of whom are treated legally as equals by the ruling authority (the fifth actor in a bargaining transaction). The main characteristic of a bargaining transaction is the formal equality between parties who *transact* the resource. Nonetheless, there are also two other types of transaction in addition to the bargaining kind of transaction. Commons identifies managerial transactions and rationing transactions (Commons 1924, 1931, 1932). While bargaining transactions involve relationships among equals, managerial and rationing transactions rest on relationships between a legal superior and a legal inferior. They thus constitute authoritative transactions. The managerial transaction is hierarchical, materialized in particular between employer and employee. In a managerial transaction, the superior is the master, manager or foreperson who gives orders to an inferior, such as a servant or worker who must obey. In such a transaction, rules must establish the usual reasonable conditions of obedience and command. While in the managerial transactions, the superior is an individual or a hierarchy of individuals giving orders that the inferior must obey, in rationing transactions, the superior is a collective superior or their official spokesperson. The rationing transaction involves the rationing of wealth or purchasing power by a superior authority, such as a legislator imposing taxes or protective tariffs or judicial decisions that transfer wealth from one individual to another. According to Commons, in modern economic life, these three types of transactions – rationing, managerial and bargaining – in their various combinations, cover the entire range of economic behaviour.

The transaction is thus a legal construct involving a transfer of economic resources. This was true for Commons as well as for Coase. Unlike Coase, Commons's institutional setting explicitly considers potential transactors (on which the opportunity costs of transactor's choices are based) and a public official actor who defines and enforces rules over transactions. Finally, different types of transactions can be identified: bargaining, managerial and rationing transactions. These types of transactions resembled, some 30 years earlier, the tripartition of Coase: market transactions, transactions within the firm and transactions by the state.

1.3. Each transaction is "coercive" – the contribution of Robert Lee Hale to transactional theory

The contributions of Robert Lee Hale (a professor of law and economics at Columbia University from 1919 through to the mid 1950s) concern the interplay of legal and economic freedoms and compulsion (cf. Fuller 1954; Samuels 1973; Duxbury 1990; Fried 1998; Mercuro *et al.* 2006; Fiorito and Vatiero 2011; Vatiero 2013). His main thesis is that economic freedom can be increased only by legal restraints on others. He then develops a theory of freedom as concealed mutual coercion.

Hale stresses that freedom is scarce, in the economic sense, and can be allocated by legal and institutional arrangements furnished by the lawmaker. He draws a fundamental distinction between voluntary and volitional freedom (see also Samuels 1973; Mercuro *et al.* 2006). Voluntary freedom is a hypothetical situation in which agents are faced merely with a scarcity of resources in nature; freedom is volitional when each choice also depends on others' choices. In other words, voluntary freedom refers to behaviours and choices that are autonomous and unconstrained by others, while volitional freedom means that behaviours and choices are limited by society – that is, by the behaviours and choices of other individuals.

Here, a parallel with John Stuart Mill's idea of liberty could be useful. Mill recognizes that each one has a set of interests. In some cases, these interests are in conflict each other (i.e., what we today call externality). In the case of conflict, the governmental intervention could be justified: "The liberty of the individual must be thus far limited; he must not make himself a nuisance to other people" (Mill 1859: Ch. 3). That is, Mill had identified an inner circle surrounding every individual as a space of complete freedom, only delimited by the absence of external consequences on someone else's identical freedom (see Giocoli 2017). For Robert Lee Hale, this inner circle would be empty or quasi, in the sense that parties' interests in economy are always in conflict with each other. Indeed, in Hale's works, actual freedom "is typically volitional and not voluntary" (Mercuro *et al.* 2006:536). Because a transaction relies on conflicting preferences and the choices of different transactors, each one involves volitional freedom: one coerces another through their choices.

Each freedom is then related to an ineradicable degree of compulsion, duress and coercion because what one party gains, the other loses (cf. Hale 1935a, 1935b, 1943; cf. also Samuels 1973). In particular, "Hale . . . chooses to see coercion where others would see freedom" (Duxbury 1990:436). Coercion is an inevitable part of all socioeconomic relationships. For this reason, Hale does not intend the term "coercion" to have negative connotations: "Coercion is not a ground for condemnation . . . hence, it seems better, in using the word "coercion," to use it in a sense which involves no moral judgment" (Hale 1923:476) or, as he points out, "to call an act coercive is not by any means to condemn it. It is because the word 'coercion' frequently seems to carry with it the stigma of impropriety, that the coercive character of so many innocent acts is so frequently denied" (Hale 1923:471). Chapter 3 develops Hale's definition of "freedom" as mutual coercion (i.e., that exercising one's own freedom necessarily entails limiting someone else's freedom), leading to the zero-sum characterization of so-called positional goods – that is, those goods for which the positive consumption by one agent is necessarily related to a negative amount of consumption by another agent.

In the Halean framework, the state does not have a passive role. As Hale emphasizes in his contributions (esp. Hale 1923, 1943, 1951, 1952), the state is also essential to the existence of individual freedoms. In Hale's words, for libertarians,

> [t]he practical function of economic theory is merely to prove to statesmen the wisdom of leaving such matters alone, not to aid them in the process of interfering. . . . But a careful scrutiny will, it is thought, reveal

a fallacy in this view, and will demonstrate that the systems advocated by professed upholders of laissez-faire are in reality permeated with coercive restrictions of individual freedom. . . . Some sort of coercive restriction of individuals, it is believed, is absolutely unavoidable

(Hale 1923:470)

As suggested by the title of one of Hale's most important works, *Freedom through Law* (1952), the state creates freedoms through legislation for one party and, consequently, legal restrictions on the freedom of other parties (cf. also Fuller 1954). For instance, "[f]reedom to drive on, before the light turns green, is restricted, but restriction serves to enhance the general freedom to drive, which would otherwise be restricted by traffic snarls" (Hale 1951:401). Again, in each market exchange, one party's consent to a transaction is extracted or obtained from the other through the market price, which the law regards as legitimate. In this respect, "every price, like every tax, is in some measure regulatory and to some extent interposes an economic impediment to the use of the article for which the price is charged" (Hale 1939:566). It also means that even if Hale does not undermine the virtues of free markets, he rejects a priori the argument that the free market was necessarily better than redistributive regulation by the state. It is thus incorrect to speak in terms of state intervention versus non-intervention. The state can permit certain freedoms for one agent and exclude by coercion the counterparty from consuming certain liberties, through law. Any particular specification of the economic system (e.g., capitalism and/or laissez-faire system) is in association with a state intervention and a particular categorization of freedoms and restraints defined and sustained by the state. Changes in an economic system are not matters of more or less state intervention but result from changes in the allocation of freedoms and restraints among individuals. The problem for the rule maker is to redistribute freedoms and legal restraints between transactors.

Hale moreover succeeds in showing the ambivalence of the law towards economic equality. On the one hand, a rule maker – if benevolent – is supposed to reduce inequality and support freedoms. On the other hand, if the freedoms of one party exist and/or accrue, then the legal restraints on a counterparty have to exist or accrue. In this respect, the law supports the freedom of one party with legal restrictions on another party. As a result, it creates or accrues inequalities in terms of legal positions, but they are necessary to create and accrue freedoms. A long passage from Hale gives more details on this issue.

At the end of the transaction, each party has lost some legal advantage which he had before, and gained some other which he did not have. As a result of past transactions, many people own property which they did not produce, many who produced material things no longer own them (if they ever did), some own much property, some little, some have large amounts of money owing to them, some are heavily burdened by debt. These *economic inequalities are embodied in legal rights* which the government enforces against others. It denies to people the liberty to make unauthorized use of an owner's property, or to deviate from obligations incurred by contract. Though the unequal property and contract rights resulted from transactions, many of the transactions were influenced by the fact that the parties were unequally hampered by the previous legal relationship.

(Hale 1951:409, italics added)

For Hale, each transaction is thus coercive. In particular, transactions are characterized by a "structure of mutual coercion," a structure which is mainly "a reflection of the particular legal rights with which the law endows [some], and the legal restrictions which it places on others" (Hale 1943:625). Such restrictions determine a degree of coercion in any transaction. Even market transactions involve several "coercive constraints" on behaviour. In this respect, Hale's contributions represent an attempt to amend the bilateral characterization of market exchange between private parties and to include the important role played by the public official in shaping and ordering transactions, in line with Commons's insights. In each transaction, the public official can furnish more freedom to one party at the cost of reducing the freedom of the other party. It also means that the public official actor can and does redistribute – rather than merely curtail – liberties.[7]

1.4.   The "specific" transaction à la Williamson

One of Williamson's main contributions was to characterize the transaction in terms of technology. First, technology defines the boundaries of a transaction: "A transaction occurs when a good or service is transferred across a technologically separable interface" (Williamson 1981:552, 1985b:179). That is, a transaction is between agents who are separated by technologically distinct stages of production, and all distinct production stages which are not separable represent all parts of the same transaction (cf. Williamson 1985a:1).

Moreover, the most important and distinctive attribute for describing a transaction derives from technological features: the asset specificity (Williamson 1981:555). Investments in specialized assets that cannot be redeployed from existing uses and users, except with a significant loss of revenue, are transaction-*specific*. There are various kinds of asset specificity (cf. Williamson 1989), such as site specificity (where successive stations are located in a cheek-by-jowl relationship to each other to economize on inventory and transportation expenses), physical asset specificity (e.g., specialized dies that are required to produce a component), human asset specificity (which arises in a learning-by-doing fashion) and dedicated assets (which are discrete investments in general-purpose plants that are made at the behest of a particular customer).

In other words, transaction-specific investments are those investments whose value in a particular transaction is greater than in the next best alternative. Note that the specificity of a transaction depends on alternatives outside the transaction and namely on the quantity and quality of potential transactors. Clearly, the notion of specific investments rests on and represents the application of a five-actors transaction à la Commons.

Contracting for goods that are produced with the support of transaction-specific assets poses serious problems. Investments in asset specificity have consequences for a firm because "such investments are also risky, since specialized assets cannot be re-employed without sacrificing their productive value if the contracts are to be interrupted or prematurely broken" (Williamson 1985a:54). With asset specificity, parties may have an interest in forming alternative-to-market arrangements in order to deal with such specific investments. There is, in other words, a problem with the *governance* of transactions. In this respect, similar to Coase, Williamson argues that "(i) markets and firms are alternative instruments for completing a related set of transactions; (ii) whether a set of transactions ought to be executed across markets or within a firm depends on the relatively efficiency of each mode" (Williamson 1975:8).

As in Coase's view, for Williamson, then, market transactions and transactions within the firm are alternative allocative mechanisms. The convenience of the former rather than the latter rests on the costs of these transactions or on an "examination of the comparative costs of planning, adapting, and monitoring task completion under alternative governance structures" (Williamson 1981:552–553). However, Williamson assumes that market transactions are the first type of transactions, while non-market transactions are only residual. In his book *Markets and Hierarchies*, Williamson indeed writes, "I assume, for expositional convenience, that 'in the beginning there was the market'" (Williamson 1975:20). This assumption is a recurrent condition of transaction cost economics; the market and market transactions are assumed to exist before other institutional alternative types of transaction (see also Hodgson 1988:177–182). This assumption that in the beginning, there was the market, as Pagano and Vatiero (2015) show, limits the analysis of the consequences of costly institutions and involves the puzzling idea that costless meta-markets are available from which to select institutions, including ordinary markets. Markets are vested with the contradictory status of being both among the costly institutions to be selected and, at the same time, the only costless institutions by which all the institutions are selected. It means losing a large part of the analysis stemming from Coase's insight into costly markets and, in general, of non-free-lunch institutions.

Despite the aforementioned limits, Williamson's theory of specific transaction has the merit, among others, to analyse together two key concepts of a transaction: adaptation and commitment. The idea of commitment in transactions relies on a mechanism that may favour cooperation even without repeated encounters. Williamson starts from the so-called "hostage model" of Schelling (1960:300) as a means to create a credible commitment and then support transactions (see Williamson 1983, 1985b). Schelling (1960) describes the example of a cooperation problem between a kidnapper who got 'cold feet' and his prisoner.

> Both the kidnapper . . . and the prisoner may search desperately for a way to commit the latter against informing on his captor. . . . If the victim has committed an act whose disclosure could lead to blackmail, he may confess it; if not, he might commit one in the presence of his captor, to create the bond that will ensure his silence.
>
> (Schelling 1960:43–44)

In other words,

> [t]he essence of these tactics is some voluntary but irreversible sacrifice of freedom of choice. They rest on the paradox that the power to constrain an adversary may depend on the power to bind oneself; that, in bargaining, weakness is often strength, freedom may be freedom to capitulate, and to burn bridges behind one may suffice to undo an opponent.
>
> (Schelling 1960:22)

Williamson develops this insight in an intermediate product market in which self-enforcing agreements involve credible commitments. In his view, efficient levels of investments, albeit in a context with incomplete contracts, can be sustained if the buyer posts/pledges a "hostage," namely something that is sacrificed in the event of the premature termination of the contract. By posting a hostage, an actor creates a commitment that serves as a safeguard for the partner's cooperation. Because the hostage is sacrificed in the termination of the relationship, this hostage has no value outside the relationship; and therefore, the hostage is ultimately a specific investment. In other words, the hostage model states that in order to foster the specific investments of one party, the other party should invest in the specific relationship.[8] Williamson maintains that one way to avoid market failure is to expand the contract relationship by devising a relationship of mutual reliance, in which the potentially opportunistic party reciprocally invests in specific capital that has value only in servicing the final demands of the product in question. If the non-salvageable value of the advance commitment undertaken by the buyer equals that of the supplier, then there will be an efficient exchange.

On the other hand, following the insights of Chester Barnard (1938), Williamson observes that the main concern of an organization is its adaptation to changing rules (Williamson 1989, 1990a). Williamson (2010:9, italics added) highlights that transaction cost economics (TCE) "has been an *exercise* in *adaptive*, intertemporal economic organization from the outset." In other words, a central problem and *exercise* in TCE is the need for an efficient adaptive mechanism of institutions. An institutional arrangement needs to be adaptive to unexpected, new circumstances in order to achieve efficiency. In the words of Williamson, "inasmuch as a full set of contingent claim markets is infeasible (by reason of bounded rationality), *adaptive*, sequential decision-making procedures need be devised" (Williamson 1973:318, italics added), and again, "[i]ntertemporal efficiency . . . requires that *adaptations* to changing market circumstances be made" (Williamson 1979:241, italics added). Namely, an efficient institutional arrangement must be such that it facilitates adaptation in the face of mutable and unpredictable ex post occurrences.[9]

A trade-off can be seen between commitment and adaptation. The former tends to create rigidity in a transaction, while the latter requires flexibility, and this trade-off in theory can and does occur. Williamson, however, shows that commitment and adaptation can work together, not in conflict, to improve a transaction. This is the case for the fundamental transformation (e.g., Williamson 1975, 1979, 1981, 1985a, 1989, 2002, 2005). The fundamental transformation is the process wherein investments in asset specificity may transform the transactional environment from an ex ante competitive market to a bilateral monopoly (see also Chapter 4). Williamson (1983, 1985a:197 ff., 1996c:124 ff.) offers petroleum exchanges as evidence of fundamental transformation.

In other words, the process of fundamental transformation is an *adaptive* process aimed at using investments in asset specificity to reconfigure an ex ante market situation where opportunism is credible towards an ex post bilateral monopoly that discourages these opportunistic behaviours and therefore creates a credible *commitment* between transactors. In the process of fundamental transformation, transactors adapt their transactions when faced with the problem of holdups. This adaptation is based on specific investments that, as hostages à la Schelling, create credible commitment.

Concluding this section, Williamson adds to transactional theory and develops the technological aspects of a transaction, especially investigating the notion of asset specificity. In this context, and using the concept of fundamental transformation, Williamson highlights the role of adaptation and credible commitments in sustaining transactions.

Notes

1 Whatever institutions are. At the beginning of his trailblazing book, *Institutions, Institutional Change and Economic Performance*, Douglass North famously states, "institutions are rules of the game in a society, or, more formally, are the humanly devised *constraints* that shape human interaction" (North 1990a:3, italics added). North repeats this idea of institutions as constraints of human behaviours in other parts of his book (e.g., North 1990a: 4) and in other works (e.g., North 1995:15). Instead, John Commons defines an institution as a "collective action in restrain, liberation and expansion of individual action" (Commons 1931:648). Note that in Commons's definition, the constraint is one of aims, but not the only aim (as North's definition seems to suggest), of institutions. Other ideas of institutions are, among others, in Hamilton (1932), Williamson (1996a), Dixit (2004) and Hodgson (2006).

2 The first Scopus document with the term "transaction" in the title, abstract or keywords is by Edward W. Bemis with an article titled "The street railway settlement in Cleveland" and published in 1908 in the *Quarterly Journal of Economics.*

3 Independently, John Dewey developed an idea of transaction which, similar to Commons's conception, is characterized by complex interactions. For instance, see Dewey and Bentley (1949).

4 For instance, when Adam Smith suggested that the pursuit of self-interest will redound to the larger interests of society via the "invisible hand" and that governmental interference with this tends to work contrary to the interests of nation, he was living in the midst of a society dominated by invasive governmental interventions, such as protective tariffs, and monopoly privileges that often generated substantial riches only for their beneficiaries. However, Smith was not a doctrinaire of laissez-faire. He also recognized that there were various governmental interventions that could improve the national welfare, if government officials were properly instructed (cf. Medema 2009).

5 Other significant answers include the following: the firm emerges in the attempt to reduce uncertainty (Knight 1921); it emerges as a device to exploit the worker (Marglin 1974); and it emerges as an organizational equilibrium of a bargaining process among corporate actors (Aoki 1984).

6 Note that, in this book, when I refer to Robinson and Friday, or to their denotations $R1$ and $F1$, I use male pronouns (he, his, him). In other cases, I use an inclusive gender-neutral language. The singular they is a widely accepted gender-neutral form.

7 In his classic text of institutional economics, *Social Control of Business* (1926), John Maurice Clark adopted Robert Lee Hale's concept of coercion.

8 A form of the hostage model has been applied in a variety of settings (Raub and Keren 1993; Anderson and Bensaou 1999; Koss 1999).

9 A similar claim is in the literature on efficient breach penalties. Because a contract that seemed sweet when agreed on may sour in the intervening interval before being enacted; the renegotiation (e.g., the breach of contractual promises) can be excusable, efficient and not immoral (see Shavell 2009; Bigoni *et al.* 2014).

2 The three dimensions of a transaction

In 1990, Williamson asked: What are principal dimensions with respect to which transactions differ? (Williamson 1990b:12) His answer (elsewhere, esp. Williamson 1985a) to this question involved identifying three key dimensions – asset specificity, uncertainty and frequency – and of the three, asset specificity is the most important and most distinctive, according to Williamson, as explained in the previous chapter. Instead, this chapter gives a different dimensionalization of transaction. Exploiting John Commons's original idea of transaction – which for Williamson is the basic unit of transaction cost economics – it introduces the three main dimensions which shape each transaction: the legal, competitive and political dimensions. The legal and political dimensions involve the relationships between each transactor and the public official. The legal dimension is on the impact of rule-making and rule-enforcing processes on transactors' choices, and the political dimension is the opposite, namely the impact of each transactor on rule-making and rule-enforcing processes via political channels. Finally, the competitive dimension concerns two issues and directions: how the market (especially through price) affects transactors' choices and – vice versa – how each transactor's choices may and do affect market configuration and prices.

2.1. The concept of transaction in the textbook perfect competition context

Let us begin with and depart from the idea of a transaction performing in a textbook perfect competition framework (cf. also Walrasian paradigm in Bowles 2004). According to the commonest interpretation of perfect competition, because their infinitely large number and their infinitely small sizes, agents, individually or in a group, cannot affect the market price and they operate in a virtually superstructure-free environment. In this context, each transactor chooses by comparing the given market price with their preferences.

The idea of a transaction in the perfect competition context thus rests on a remarkable conceptualization of an important limiting case: each individual transactor, actual or potential, is a price taker. This means in our transaction between the agent $R1$ and the agent $F1$ that the price of a *widget* is set by the remaining whole market, which comprises an infinitely large number of anonymous alternative sellers (denoted by a "representative agent" $R2$) and an infinitely large number of anonymous alternative buyers (analogously represented by $F2$). For instance, if the agent $R1$ offers the widget at a higher price than is the market price, then the buyer $F1$, if rational, will be – in a perfect competition framework – free and will prefer to purchase the widget from $R1$'s competitors, namely by the representative agent $R2$. If the agent $R1$ wants to sell their widget, he thus needs to reduce the price to the given market price.

This also means that the market (composed of potential counterparties and competitors of two transactors) has a one-directional influence over the actual transaction between transactor $R1$ and transactor $F1$. This is shown in Figure 2.1 by an arrow from the representative alternative transactors $R2$ and $F2$ to the actual transactor $R1$. Hereinafter, for the sake of simplicity, we focus on the transactor $R1$; however, an analogous effect also holds true for the other transactors, for example, $F1$.

Nevertheless, this idea of a transaction as coming from the perfect competition framework has (at least) three limitations:

1   There is no room for the intervention/interference of an external party (i.e., a public official actor, a legislature, or governmental bureau) to define, inter alia, who is allowed to transact, what constitutes a legal transaction, how transactions are enforced, etc.
2   It deprives a transactor in the marketplace of any impact on prices as well as the total produced quantities, technologies or actions of others. Even if there is a wide variety of competitive strategies that rest on the potential to affect and reconfigure the market and its prices, such as advertising, making product innovation, training workers, raising rivals' costs, etc., these strategies find little to no rationale in the perfect competition model, where all prices are exogenous.
3   Lastly, transactors are not interested in acting, alone or in groups, in order to seek favourable changes in laws and regulations. That is, transactors do not have the incentives of influencing, mainly via polity, the rule-making and/or rule-enforcing processes.

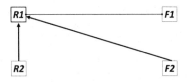

Figure 2.1 The idea of transaction in the perfect competition framework.

In summary, the idea of a transaction embedded in a perfect competition context casts little to no light on the legal (point 1), competitive (point 2) or political (point 3) factors that by contrast characterize all transactions in the real world (Demsetz 1982 advances a similar critique). Departing from these three limits of the perfect competition model, this chapter now introduces three dimensions of transaction in the real world: the legal, competitive and political dimensions.

2.2.   Introducing the legal dimension of a transaction

The assumption of price taking in the perfect competition framework is also pervasive throughout Coase's (1960) entire argument and, in particular, the Coase theorem. For instance, in the famous example of the rancher's herd that invades the farmer's land, Coase writes,

> It might be thought the fact that the cattle-raiser would pay for all crops damaged would lead the farmer to increase his planting if a cattle-raiser came to occupy the neighbouring property. But this is not so. If the crop was previously sold *in conditions of perfect competition*, marginal cost was equal to price for the amount of planting undertaken and any expansion would have reduced the profits of the farmer. . . . Of course, if cattle-raising commonly involved the destruction of crops, the coming into existence of a cattle-raising industry might raise the price of the crops involved and farmers would then extend their planting. But I wish to confine my attention to the individual farmer.
>
> (Coase 1960:3–4, italics added)

And again:

> I think it is clear that if the cattle-raiser is liable for damage caused and the pricing system works smoothly, the reduction in the value of production elsewhere will be taken into account in computing additional cost involved in increasing the size of the herd. This cost will be weighed against the value of the additional meat production and, *given perfect competition* in the cattle industry, the allocation of resources in cattle-raising will be optimal.
>
> (Coase 1960:5, italics added)

Hence, it is not accidental that in the first version of the theorem, as formulated by Stigler, this assumption is made clear: "The Coase theorem . . . asserts that under *perfect competition*, private and social costs will be equal" (Stigler 1966:113, italics added).

If one pays more attention to Ronald Coase's words in his contributions, however, one can clearly see that the legal dimension of a transaction represents the main difference between Coase's argument and the perfect competition context:

> It is necessary to know whether the damaging business is liable or not for damage caused since without *the establishment of this initial delimitation of rights* there can be no market transactions to transfer and recombine them. But the ultimate result (which maximizes the value of production) is independent of the legal position if the pricing system is assumed to work without cost.
>
> (Coase 1960:8, italics added)

In this passage, Coase identifies two hypotheses and two theses of what was called the Coase theorem – despite this, there is not consensus on statements of the Coase theorem (in particular, see the excellent history of the Coase theorem in Medema 2017):

> Hypothesis 1: Null transaction costs ("the pricing system is assumed to work without costs").
>
> Hypothesis 2: A clear definition – by *someone* – of property rights ("the establishment of this initial delimitation of rights").
>
> Thesis 1 (the so-called efficiency thesis): The price mechanism attains efficiency ("the ultimate result . . . maximizes the value of production").
>
> Thesis 2 (the so-called invariant thesis): Efficiency is attained independently of the initial allocation of rights ("the ultimate result . . . is independent of the legal position").

What is important here is that, according to the Coase theorem, the Pareto-optimum which the market may achieve (Thesis 1) depends on two conditions (Hypotheses 1 and 2). One is the famous transaction cost null assumption (Hypothesis 1). The second one is that "someone," a public official actor, has to define and enforce rights (Hypothesis 2). Market transactions thus cannot exist without an institutional structure in place which indicates property rights, i.e., who has the *claim* to be paid in a particular transaction and who has the *duty* to pay whom in the same transaction – note the *correlative* claim–duty (it will be developed in Chapter 3).

One consequence is that "[t]he assignment of a right to one party simultaneously exposes others to the effects of the exercise of that right" (Medema 2009:105). Looking at this from an economic perspective, the definition of property rights over economic resources creates economic rivalry among parties and, if transaction costs are null, this economic rivalry begets the efficient final allocation of rights and related economic resources.

Although questionable (cf. Hodgson 2015; Medema 2017; Arruñada 2017; Deakin *et al*. 2017; Smith 2017), the difference between the Coase theorem world[1] and the perfect competition framework is represented by this legal dimension, consisting of the active role of the public official actor in defining and enforcing rights. In particular, according to Coase's argument, the public official actor has to structure institutions in order to reduce the costs of transactions. In Coase's words,

> For anything approaching perfect competition to exist, an intricate system of rules and regulations would normally be needed. Economists observing the regulations of the exchanges often assume that they represent an attempt to exercise monopoly power and aim to restrain competition. They ignore or, at any rate, fail to emphasize an alternative explanation for these regulations: that they exist *in order to reduce transaction costs* and therefore to increase the volume of trade.
>
> (Coase 1988:9, italics added)

Economic institutions thus have the main purpose and effect of economizing on transaction costs (see esp. Williamson 1985a). A concrete example of this role of the public official is in Coase's (1959) "The Federal Communications Commission," where he demonstrates that efficiency in the allocation of radio frequencies can be improved if the public official defines clear property rights on the radio frequency spectrum.[2] More generally, a normative corollary to the Coase theorem is that the law (especially property rights and contract law) should be designed by a public official actor to lower transaction costs and facilitate efficient outcomes. In doing so, the Coase theorem extends the idea of the transaction in the perfect competition framework, recognizing the role (even if limited) of the legal dimension of a transaction.

Stylizing this idea of transaction, the transactor $R1$ is affected by the public official P. Indeed, although the final result when transaction costs are null is independent of how the public official actor P assigns property rights (invariant thesis), an initial definition of property rights by P (Hypothesis 2) is needed to achieve efficiency (efficiency thesis). Without rights, transactors or potential transactors are not able to act on their preferences, which is to say that the transactional outcome is a function of rights structure, in the sense that it depends on an initial definition and real enforcement of (property) rights.

Figure 2.2 shows the resulting idea of transaction. The one-directional arrow from the alternatives ($R2$ and $F2$) towards the actual transactor $R1$ denotes that the market has an impact on the actual transaction, as in the perfect competition context in Figure 2.1. However, unlike the perfect competition model, the one-directional (gray) arrow from public official P to the actual transactor $R1$ indicates that, as introduced by the Coasian argument, the public official also plays a role in all transactional outcomes and therefore

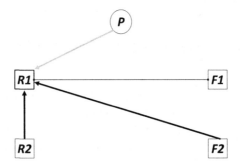

Figure 2.2 The transaction in Coase theorem.

affects the choices of transactor *R*1 – reminding us again that the definition of rights is necessary, even if it is invariant for efficiency.

Although it is more complex than the idea in the perfect competition context is, the conceptualization of a transaction in the Coase theorem has (at least) two important limits:

1   Each transactor is (still, as in perfect competition) a price taker. This means that while the transaction between agent *R*1 and agent *F*1 depends on the market price, their choices do not seem to affect the market price or market configuration.[3] For instance, the externality between the rancher and the farmer – the invasion of the rancher's herd onto farmer's land – does not affect any other alternative relationships. Indeed, in the rancher–farmer example, the market price of the crops (from which derives the marginal value of crops destroyed by rancher's herd) is *given* and equal to $1 per ton both before and after the definition of property rights and the solution of externality (cf. Coase 1960:3–5). The theory of incomplete contracts and specific investments relaxes this assumption.

2   Each transactor is a rule taker. Transactors seem to be unable to affect or to be uninterested in affecting the rule-making and rule-enforcing processes. For instance, the farmer and the rancher cannot be, or are not interested in changing, according to their preferences, the initial assignment of rights as determined by rule maker *P*, even if the initial allocation of rights affects the final distribution of the parties' wealth (*who pays whom*). The so-called political-transaction-costs perspective removes this assumption.

The rest of this chapter and the book relax these two assumptions.

2.3. Introducing the competitive dimension of a transaction

A consequence of the assumption of the perfect competition framework is that agents by definition cannot affect the market configuration and market prices. Incomplete contract theory removes this assumption; namely, the relationship between a transactor and their competitors takes place in two directions.

Consider a typical setting, where agent $R1$ makes a specific investment to improve the widget that is sold to agent $F1$. In an incomplete contract framework, a transaction works under two conditions:

1   A costly enforcement by the public official actor P: The observation by the public official of the conduct of transactors and even their punishment in the case of violation of the agreement is costly. Enforcement is thus fallible.
2   The asymmetric nature of asset specificity: Because specific investments have little to no value outside a relationship but great value within it, investor $R1$ is locked in the relationship with agent $F1$ and, therefore, cannot move from the specific relationship with $F1$ to outside options in the spot market (e.g., to the alternative buyer, $F2$). On the contrary, non-investor $F1$ can opportunistically and credibly threaten to switch to the spot market (i.e., to the alternative seller, $R2$) if the contract and agreed surplus-sharing rule do not change.

This exposes the investor to the adverse renegotiation of the counterparty of the original agreed-on terms, namely there is a risk of ex post opportunistic renegotiation (i.e., holdup) that diminishes incentives for specific investments. Both the public official P with their fallible enforcement and the asymmetry of alternatives in the outside market affect the choices of investing transactor $R1$. In this context, the investor ($R1$) has reasons to underinvest in asset specificity.

Two main notable remedies are proposed by the literature:

1   the assignment of residual control rights (esp. Hart 1995; see also Hart 2017)
2   the process of fundamental transformation (e.g., Williamson 1975, 1979, 1981, 1985a, 1989, 2002, 2005; see also Klein 1996).

Interestingly, both remedies aim at alleviating the asymmetry of market alternatives.

The solution proposed by Oliver Hart and his coauthors (the Grossman–Hart–Moore model) is based on the fact that the allocation of residual control rights modifies outside market alternatives. Consider the famous textbook case of Fisher Body and General Motors. In 1919, General Motors agreed to purchase metal car bodies exclusively from Fisher Body. When the contract between Fisher Body and General Motors was entered into in 1919, the dominant production process for automobiles consisted of individually constructed open bodies; the closed metal bodies supplied by Fisher Body were essentially a novelty. After 1919, demand for closed metal bodies grew dramatically, and by 1924, they accounted for about two-thirds of automobile sales of General Motors. General Motors therefore encouraged Fisher Body to increase its capacity. Fisher Body's resistance to make a specific investment, that is, to build a factory near General Motors operations, prompted General Motors to buy Fisher Body. Namely, General Motors acquired residual control rights over Fisher Body's assets:

> once General Motors owns Fisher Body and Fisher becomes an employee of General Motors, Fisher can no longer take advantage of an imperfect contract to threaten nonperformance because the ultimate power to make most important investment and management decisions, such as the location of the auto-body production plant, is legally transferred to the employer/owner [General Motors]. . . . The reduction in the ability of employees to threaten nonperformance can be seen clearly if we consider the possibility of bribes or side payments by third parties to influence an employee's plant-location decision. While an independent contractor has the right (and even the duty to its shareholders) to consider such payments in making decisions, employees cannot do so.
>
> (Klein and Murphy 1997:418)

The allocation of residual control rights saves transaction costs deriving from ex post opportunism or holdup because the potential opportunistic party, say $F1$, has no means to (threaten to) switch on the alternatives in the outside market (say $R2$) given that his physical assets are, after the vertical integration, under the control of the other party, that is $R1$. Namely, $F1$ is, after the integration, a branch of $R1$ and a renegotiation (holdup) is no longer credible.

As we argue in depth in Chapter 4, the allocation of residual control rights affects competitors and competition. For instance, in the case of Fisher Body and General Motors, the acquisition of Fisher Body by General Motors not only transformed the relationship between General Motors and Fisher Body (which was influenced by the risk of holdup) but also dramatically changed the conditions of competition in the market, raising the costs of General Motors' rivals. This means that the choice of a transactor to acquire a counterparty's physical assets (i.e., vertical integration) mitigates the holdup problem but also affects the market, its configuration and consequently its

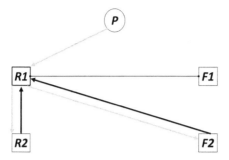

Figure 2.3 The transaction in the incomplete contract theory.

prices. In Figure 2.3, the arrow between the transactor *R*1 and alternative transactors (*R*2 and *F*2) is therefore bidirectional. It indicates not only that the rest of the market affects, especially via price, the transaction and transactor's choices, as in the perfect competition model, but also that the choices of transactors (e.g., vertical integration) have an impact on the market and its configuration. It is indeed not surprisingly that in the antitrust cases of vertical integration, antitrust authorities consider both aspects: the harm coming from lessening competition (the so-called efficiency offence) and the efficiency-improvement coming from the alleviation of the problem of holdup (the so-called efficiency defence). And, it is not surprising that the forerunner of this kind of economic analysis concerning both the "monopoly branch" and the "efficiency branch" was Williamson (1985a:23–29).

Williamson indeed proposes a somewhat different way to mitigate the risk of holdup. He advances the idea that specific investments may reduce the field of available alternatives for transactors from a large number (i.e., the ex ante bargaining situation) to a small number (i.e., the ex post bidding bilateral monopoly). That is, because each transaction among parties creates a transactional residual that favours a continued bilateral trading relationship, specific investments affect alternatives in the outside market. In particular, the specific investment of *R*1 plays a commitment role that makes it costly for non-investor *F*1 to switch to faceless alternatives in outside market *R*2. More specifically, Williamson's idea is that specific investments may achieve the transformation, which Williamson calls the fundamental transformation, of the transactional environment from an ex ante competitive market to a bilateral monopoly. Williamson writes,

> [t]he Fundamental Transformation applies to that subset of transactions for which large numbers of qualified suppliers at the outset are

transformed into what, in effect, is a *bilateral* exchange relation during contract execution and at the contract renewal interval. . . . The key factor in determining whether a large numbers supply condition will *evolve* into a bilateral exchange relation is the degree to which the transaction in question *is supported by durable investments in transaction-specific assets.*

(Williamson 2002:176, italics added)

Such a transformation of market alternatives therefore reduces non-investor exit options and decreases the risk of opportunistic behaviours.

It also means that specific investments play a double role:

1   They are the origin of the problem of holdup as suggested in the standard literature.
2   They (may) create a credible commitment that mitigates the problem of holdup.

This double role for specific investments is also noted by Williamson:

[c]redible commitments and credible threats share this common attribute: Both appear in conjunction with irreversible, specialized investments. But whereas credible commitments are undertaken in support of alliance and to promote exchange, credible threats appear in the context of conflict and rivalry.

(Williamson 1985a:167)

In both the Grossman–Hart–Moore model and the notion of fundamental transformation, alternatives in the outside market play a key role: for opportunistic behaviours (i.e., holdup) to be credible, the non-investor should be *credibly* able to switch to alternatives in the outside market (e.g., the spot market of the "widget"). Considering Hart's and Williamson's arguments, potential alternatives $R2$ and $F2$ to an actual transaction between agent $R1$ and agent $F1$ play an essential role not only in the emergence of opportunistic behaviour – the credibility of holdup depends on the asymmetry of outside options – but also in its remedies – particularly the remedies to holdup needed to foreclose the market competition. An ex ante competitive configuration in which the non-investor $F1$ has available alternative counterparties (e.g., $R2$) to the specific relationship (and therefore a credible threat of renegotiation) is modified for the allocation of residual control rights or for the process of fundamental transformation in an ex post configuration in which switching to alternatives is costly or impossible. Figure 2.3 shows this idea of transaction through the gray arrows. The choice of $R1$ to acquire the physical assets of $F1$ – that is, vertical integration à la Hart – or to invest in asset specificity leading to a Williamsonian process of fundamental transformation has effects on alternatives $R2$ and $F2$ (gray arrows), competition and market prices.

Note that although sometimes one hears the claim that the Grossman–Hart–Moore model formalized Williamson's contributions, in reality Grossman–Hart–Moore and Williamson offer different theories, which are essentially orthogonal (e.g., Gibbons 2005). In Grossman–Hart–Moore, specific investments are *solely* the origin of the problem of the holdup, and the assignment of residual control rights is one of remedies. Instead, Williamson argues that specific investments are still one of conditions of the emergence of holdup but that they may *also* transform the configuration of alternatives in the outside market and therefore mitigate the holdup problem.[4] We develop these insights in Chapter 4.

2.4.   Introducing the political dimension of a transaction

Individuals may derive benefits from institutions and rules that are more consistent with their interests, as originally noted by Thorstein Veblen (e.g., 1899, 1923) and John Commons (esp. Commons 1924, 1950, 1959) and more recently by Mancur Olson (1965, 1982), Douglass North (1990a, 1990b) and Avinash Dixit (1996). The general idea is that "if rents are not perfectly allocated ex ante by contracts and rules, there is ample space for economic actors to exert pressure on the regulatory, judiciary, and political system to grab a larger share of these rents" (Zingales 2017:119). In this respect, transactors are not rule takers or institution takers, but they can devise them. Commons uses what he calls the artificial selection theory of institutional evolution (à la Veblen[5]) to demonstrate that each institution originates in the creative attempts by transactors to advance their purposes as they interact with one another (Commons 1924). For an institution to emerge and persist, a particular pattern of interaction must prove successful enough and meet with the approval of those who possess the power to permit or forbid the pattern of action. Neither polity nor economy are given, independent and self-sufficient, but both thus emerge through a process of coevolution. Both economy and its legal foundations are outcomes of an ongoing interaction between interest groups competing and cooperating in a world of scarcity.

For instance, consider Demsetz's (1967) example on the introduction of property rights to Native American tribes inhabiting Canada's Labrador Peninsula – though Demsetz's interpretation of the example is highly debatable (e.g., see Bromley 1989). Because the commercial fur trade with European settlers developed in the early 1700s changed the demand for furs and the rewards from hunting, these communities called to the "local rule maker" for a system of private hunting territories. For a scarcity problem of resources, individuals demanded that the local public official delimit property rights over the land (Demsetz 1967). In her recent book (2019, ch. 2), Katharina Pistor illustrates a further example concerning land legislation. She notes that while in British North American colonies the law since 1732 (Debt Recovery Act) gave to creditors the right to seize all debtor's land, including family estates, and to put it on the auction block, in England these norms waited until 1881. She explains that because British elites were landowners in England and creditors in British colonies, English voters demanded politicians enact such a land legislation only in colonies, but much later at home.

> English lawmakers did not lack knowledge about alternatives to the complex land conveyance regime that solicitors had piece together for wealthy families; they lacked the political will to implement them. The calculus in the colonies was different. There, the English legislature had few qualms about shifting the balance of power from owners to creditors; to state the obvious, in most cases the creditors in question were Englishmen.
>
> (Pistor 2019:40)

Both in Demsetz's and in Pistor's examples, rules are not given, but people can ask for their changes via political channels. Douglass North captures something close to this idea of a political dimension of transaction:

> institutions are not necessarily or even usually created to be socially efficient, rather they . . . are created to serve the interests of those with the bargaining power to devise [the] new rule. In a zero-transaction-cost world, bargaining strength does not affect the efficiency of outcomes, but in a world of positive transaction costs it does and given the *lumpy* indivisibilities that characterize institutions, it shapes the direction of long-run economic change.
>
> (North 1990a:16, italics in original)

In particular, transactors can affect rule-making and rule-enforcing processes through several political channels. Among other things, the transactor can be a member of interest groups designed to "capture" the rule maker (Stigler 1971), the rule enforcer (Landes and Posner 1975) and the regulator (Spiller 2013). Another political channel for the transactor is the vote: each transactor in a democratic nation is a voter, or in an extreme example, they can represent the median voter who determines elections and may affect the institutional setting (Culpepper 2011). A further alternative is that the transactor contributes to the formation of ideologies, which, as the literature suggests, affect polity and therefore legislation (e.g., Roe 1994, 2003).

This political influence can have both positive and negative effects on transactional outcomes. In a positive view, Commons (1924, 1950, 1959) affirmed that pressure groups, and especially the labour unions, farm organizations and cooperatives, were the most vital institutions in society and the lifeblood of democracy. According to Commons, the freedom to form pressure groups mattered more than any of the other democratic freedoms. However, there are also sceptical views. Olson (1965, 1982) has suggested that collective actions and the growth of special interest groups result in unproductive competition to capture rents, which do not add up to social well-being. According to Olson, there is a *surprising and systematic tendency for the exploitation* (Olson 1965:3, 28, 35) of the great group (i.e., society) by the small subgroup (e.g., pressure groups). Similarly, Acemoglu and Robinson (2012) argue that inclusive or extractive institutions derive from the political dimension of a transaction. Inclusive economic institutions are those that allow and encourage participation by the great mass of people in economic activities that make best use of their talents and skills and that enable individuals to make the choice they wish. Inclusive economic institutions foster economic activity, productivity growth and economic prosperity. Instead, extractive economic institutions – extractive because such institutions are designed to extract incomes and wealth from one subset of society to benefit a different subset – have opposite properties to those that are called inclusive.

Even taking a positive view into consideration, however, since transactors can affect the political arena and then rule-making and rule-enforcing processes, there is a problem of political commitment. The Coase theorem assumes that transactors can commit to their agreements because transactors rely on binding agreements enforced by public official *P*, but such an assumption is not granted. For instance, Robert Cooter (1987) observes that one of the most relevant impediments to the working of the Coase theorem in the political domain is the existence of uncertainties regarding the content and enforceability of rights. Similarly, extending the Coase theorem to the political sphere, Daron Acemoglu defines political Coase theorem as the view that "political and economic transactions create a strong tendency towards policies and institutions that achieve the best outcomes given the varying needs and requirements of societies, *irrespective of who, or which social group, has political power*" (Acemoglu 2003:621, italics added). Acemoglu presents a formal political economy model in which social conflict and limited commitment are the key factors that undermine the validity of the political Coase theorem.

The main consequence is what Weingast calls the fundamental political dilemma of an economic system:

> A government strong enough to protect property rights and enforce contracts is also strong enough to confiscate the wealth of its citizens. Thriving markets require not only the appropriate system of property rights and a law of contracts, but a secure political foundation that limits the ability of the state to confiscate wealth. Far from obvious, however, are the circumstances that produce a political system that plays one role instead of the other.
>
> (Weingast 1995:1)

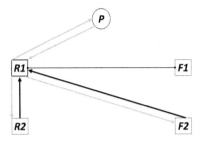

Figure 2.4 Each trans-actor is also a political actor.

The commitment problem relies on the fact that the state, with its monopoly of legitimate coercive power, can enforce contracts and rights *and* can use its power to renege on promises and change the terms of contracts and rights. This commitment problem may render transactional outcomes risky and uncertain and, therefore, restrict transactions. Therefore, the wise Machiavellian prince should be one who seeks to give and ensure credible commitments (Williamson 1996c).

An answer to the commitment problem of the polity comes from so-called ordoliberalism. Ordoliberals (the main exponents were Walter Eucken and Franz Bohm) were European intellectuals who developed an original view on liberalism before and just after the turn of the twentieth century, with ideas closely associated with the Vienna Circle of intellectuals, and in Germany via the Freiburg School (cf. among others Gerber 1998; Felice and Vatiero 2014; Vatiero 2010a, 2015). There is a strict connection in this approach between political and economic order (*ordo*). The ordoliberal solution to the political commitment problem was to embed the market in a "constitutional" framework that would protect the process of competition from distortion by transactors' private power. The rigidity of an economic constitution ensures a stable institutional context characterized, among other things, by independent authorities (especially in the field of economic transactions).

In any case, because transactors who interact in a transaction may also contend with or coalesce in the political arena to align the laws and rules of transaction with their interests and preferences, each transactor has an effect on public official *P*, as the gray arrow in Figure 2.4 indicates. This means that public official actor *P* affects transactor behaviour (as in Coase's argument), but transactors may also affect rule-making or rule-enforcing processes via political channels.

2.5.   What should be next? Go back to the past

Because this is a complex construct, a more comprehensive conceptualization of the transaction, which is able to take into account and combine legal,

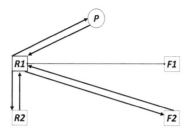

Figure 2.5 A broader idea of transaction.

competitive and political factors, is fundamental. This book uses the idea of a transaction as originally formulated by John Commons. Accordingly, the transactional outcome is the result not only of the actions and promises of actual transactors but also of the expected actions held by potential transactors, and it is also influenced by the power of the legal system. In addition, each actor affects every other actor (see Figure 2.5).

This multifaceted idea of transaction has the advantage of allowing one to take into account the three dimensions of a transaction: the legal dimension (i.e., the role of public actor P in a transaction and in transactor's choices), the competitive dimension (i.e., the effects of one transactor's choices on potential transactors) and the political dimension (which concerns the transactor as a political actor).

Notes

1 Although the world of the Coase theorem "has often been described as a Coasian world," Coase writes:

> Nothing could be further from the truth. It is the world of modern economic theory, one which I was hoping to persuade economists to leave. what I did in 'The problem of social cost' was simply to bring to light some of its properties
> (Coase 1988:174)

In particular, "[i]n an economic theory which assumes that transaction costs are non-existent, markets have no function to perform" (Coase 1988:7–8). And, "it seems perfectly reasonable to develop the theory of exchange by an elaborate analysis of individuals exchanging nuts for apples on the edge of the forest or some similar fanciful example" (Coase 1988:9).

2 As Medema (2009, 2017) reports, a group of about 20 economists from Chicago, including Milton Friedman and George Stigler, met with Coase for the purpose of discussing on Coase's fallacious analysis in "The Federal Communications Commission." Nevertheless, Coase persuaded other economists and he was pushed to write a fuller treatment of his argumentation in "The problem of social costs."

3 One related problem in Coase's analysis is that he confined his attention to two-party disputes, e.g., the farmer and the rancher; the railway emitting sparks and the owner of an adjacent woodlot; the keeper of coney-burrows and the farmer; and the parties

in the nineteenth-century nuisances cases (see Merrill and Smith 2001a:371; see also Merrill and Smith 2001b). The focus on two parties implied imagining the property as right in personam and not as right in rem as is usually considered by legal analysis (see Arruñada 2017). An interesting attempt to extend Coasian approach on bilateral relationships to multi-tier settings such as global value chains is in Bellantuono (2019).

4 For instance, Williamson (2000:605) points out:

> The most consequential difference between the TCE [transaction cost economics] and GHM [Grossman–Hart–Moore] setups is that the former holds that maladaptation in the contract execution interval is the principal source of inefficiency, whereas GHM vaporize ex post maladaptation by their assumptions of common knowledge and costless bargaining.

5 Thorstein Veblen originally introduces the idea of an institutional evolution. In 1899, Veblen states that the evolution of institutions is a process of endless selective adaptation: institutions modify, develop and adapt to changing circumstances and, in particular, to the habits of the thought of individuals which make up the community (Veblen 1899, especially Chapter VIII).

3 The legal dimension of transactions

We saw in the previous chapter that the idea of a transaction in the perfect competition framework is characterized by the limiting assumption that there is no room for any intervention or interference of a public official to define, for instance, who is allowed to transact, what constitutes a transaction, etc. Coase adds the legal dimension of a transaction to the perfect competition framework. One key point of his argument is that the definition of rights is a necessary pre-condition in order to ensure Pareto-efficiency in a market transaction (cf. Hypothesis 2 of the Coase theorem). Otherwise, without such a clear definition of rights over resources, externalities (namely the misallocation of resources) will persist. This chapter is about the definition of rights. It develops the concept of the adversarial nature of legal positions – as originally introduced by Wesley N. Hohfeld and reformulated by John Commons – using the concept of positional goods. The main finding of this chapter is that for the adversarial (or positional) nature of legal positions, the definition of (property) rights by a public official is never neutral and costless, as instead is suggested by the invariant thesis of the Coase theorem.

However, this chapter does not investigate a second (but important) aspect of the legal dimension of transactions: the enforcement of rights. Although in Coase (1960) they seem to coincide, in the real world, the definition of rights (rule-making process) and their enforcement (rule-enforcing process) represent two distinctive issues. Indeed, a clear definition of contents of property rights is not sufficient if rights are *badly* enforced. In the clear words of Tullock (1980:659),

> [i]n discussing the efficiency of the law there are two quite different problems. The first is whether the law itself is well designed to achieve goals that society regards as desirable. The second is whether the process of enforcing of law is efficient.

According to the literature, poorly enforcing rights over economic transactions weakens incentives to invest and has a negative impact on economic growth (North 1990a; Acemoglu *et al.* 2001; Acemoglu and Johnson 2005). Empirical works offer evidence that fallible or bad enforcement negatively impacts economic transactions (e.g., Visaria 2009; Chemin 2009a, 2009b, 2012; Ponticelli and Alencar 2016). This chapter is dedicated solely to the definition and contents of rights, while Chapter 4 deals with incomplete contract theory, which assumes, among other things, a context of positive and marginally relevant enforcement costs.

3.1. The adversarial (or "positional") nature of legal positions

Yale Law Professor Wesley Newcomb Hohfeld is generally regarded as a forerunner of legal realism, and in two seminal articles published in 1913 and 1917, he offered a paradigmatic taxonomy of legal positions that is particularly influential for interwar American institutionalist figures, including John Commons and Robert Lee Hale (see Fiorito 2010; Vatiero 2010b; Fiorito and Vatiero 2011), and for the approach to the bundle of rights which characterizes Coasian literature (e.g., Merrill and Smith 2001a, 2001b). According to Hohfeld (1913, 1917), there are eight fundamental conceptions, *the lowest common denominator*, through which all legal problems can be stated: claim, privilege, power or immunity, on one hand, and their correlatives, duty, no-right, liability and disability, on the other. The correlative nature of legal positions means that each legal position is available to an individual if, and only if, a corresponding, correlative legal position is occupied by some other individual. John Commons developed Hohfeld's concepts of legal positions in 1924, within the pages of his *Legal Foundations of Capitalism* – it suggests that Commons considered Hohfeld's jural relations formulation as a component of his own transactional economic framework (cf. Fiorito 2010; Vatiero 2010b; Fiorito and Vatiero 2011). On purely terminological grounds, Commons adopted the word "liberty," whereas Hohfeld used "privilege." Commons points out that the term "liberty" is to be preferred as the general legal opposite of duty, since the term "privilege" is used in law to refer to those situations where the existence of a duty that is present in the standard case is negated by a particular legal defence or unique circumstance. Finally, Commons substitutes the term "exposure" for Hohfeld's "no-right" (see also Fiorito 2010; Vatiero 2010b; Fiorito and Vatiero 2011).

The representation of legal correlatives in Table 3.1 is based on Commons's development of Hohfeld's original formulation. All legal problems

Table 3.1 Legal correlatives.

Transactor	Jural or legal correlatives			
	Exogenous/external enforcement		*Endogenous/internal enforcement*	
R1	Claim	Liberty	Power	Immunity
F1	Duty	Exposure	Liability	Disability

may be described through four pairs of jural correlatives: claim–duty, liberty–exposure, power–liability and immunity–disability.

- *Claim–duty correlative.* A *claim* (or right, in the strict sense) means that agent $R1$ has a state-sanctioned assurance (namely that there is an enforcement by public official actor P) that agent $F1$ will behave in a certain way towards agent $R1$. However, this occurs if, and only if, agent $F1$ has the *duty* to engage in such behaviour with respect to agent $R1$; that is, a duty is the legal position of agent $F1$, who is commanded by society (via the power of public official P) to act for the benefit of agent $R1$ and who will be penalized by society (namely by public official P) for disobedience. The correlative of a claim is thus a duty. For instance, if $R1$ has a claim, enforced by public official P, that $F1$ pays a price for using $R1$'s materials and instruments, then $F1$ has the duty to pay that price.
- *Liberty–exposure correlative. Liberty* is one's freedom from the claim of someone else. Agent $R1$ has the liberty to behave in a certain way towards agent $F1$ if and only if agent $F1$ is exposed to not having the aid of the public official P to prevent agent $R1$ from behaving in a certain way. *Exposure* is the legal correlative of the liberty of another party. For instance, for an easement of access, agent $R1$ has liberty to enter $F1$'s land; namely, $F1$ is exposed to the fact that the public official actor will not stop $R1$'s access.
- *Power–liability correlative. Power* is the legal ability to undertake certain acts that alter legal relations. Agent $R1$'s power arises when $R1$'s own voluntary act causes new legal relations between agent $R1$ and agent $F1$, against agent $F1$'s will. Whenever a power exists, there is at least one other human being whose legal relationship will be altered when the power is exercised. The person whose legal relationship will be altered is under a *liability*. For instance, in the scenario that agent $R1$ is an employer and agent $F1$ his employee, no external party (P) intervenes to stimulate the maximum effort of worker $F1$, but the entrepreneur $R1$ needs to create an effective incentive scheme to push agent $F1$ to work as agent $R1$ wants. If agent $R1$ is able to provide such an incentive scheme, then agent $R1$ will "alter" the relationship with $F1$ according to $R1$'s preferences. $R1$ is exercising a power.
- *Immunity–disability correlative.* Finally, *immunity* is any legal situation in which a given relationship vested in one person cannot be changed by the acts of another person. Correlatively, the one who lacks the ability to alter the other individual's legal position is said to be under a *disability*. This means that if agent $R1$ is not able to provide an incentive scheme for the employment relationship with agent $F1$, then agent $F1$ will be immune from agent $R1$.

Note that the claim–duty correlative is similar to the power–liability correlative in terms of material consequences. Who has a claim, analogously to who has a power, can mean that the other party performs as they prefer. The only difference is that in the claim–duty correlative the enforcement is external or exogenous (via the public official *P*), whereas in the power–liability correlative the legal relation is based on an endogenous, internal enforcement. The legal position of power is thus a sort of legal position of claim but without the active aid of the law, society or a public official. In a power–liability correlative, the agent needs to "invest" in the relationship to alter the relation as they prefer (e.g., through an incentive scheme). Similarly, the legal position of immunity is a sort of liberty but without the active aid of a public official. While the first pair of correlatives – that is, claim–duty correlative and liberty–exposure correlative – is enforced with the active aid of the law, namely externally, exogenously by the public official *P*, the second two correlatives – that is, power–liability and immunity–disability – are thus characterized by an endogenous, internal enforcement (though within the exogenous legal limits), as in Table 3.1.

Moreover, because legal entitlements may and do also come into conflict, for individual interests, legal correlatives are adversarial in nature. The legal position (e.g., claim, liberty and power) of *R*1 is against *F*1's legal position (respectively, duty, exposure and liability). For instance, the set of actions that defines the claims of agent *R*1 imposes duties on some individual – that is, agent *F*1. A jural relationship is indeed formed by one advantaged party, in our case the transactor *R*1, called *dominus*, and a disadvantaged counterparty, in our case the transactor *F*1, called *servus*. This brings about the consumption of legal positions with opposite signs: the claim by agent *R*1, as his *desired output*, and the duty of agent *F*1, as his *costly input*. In a similar manner, the power–liability relationship consists of agent *R*1's benefit (i.e., the power) and of agent *F*1's cost (i.e., liability). Any utility deriving from rights and powers must therefore jointly relate to a disutility deriving from duties and liabilities (see Table 3.2).

Because of their adversarial nature, the legal relationship scheme overlaps with the characterization of positional goods (cf. Pagano 1999; Vatiero 2013; Pagano and Vatiero 2019). A positional good is an "economic" good of which the consumption/utility is zero-sum (cf. Pagano 1999; Hopkins and Kornienko 2004). Similarly, legal positions inevitably involve consumption and utilities with opposite signs. *Everyone* cannot consume claims, liberties,

Table 3.2 The adversarial nature of legal positions (from Pagano and Vatiero 2019).

Claim/power	Duty/disability
Benefits	Costs
Desired output	Costly input
Utility	Disutility

powers and immunities; for some individuals, the exercise of these jural positions must imply the exercise of "unfavourable" correlative legal positions, that is, duties, exposures, liabilities and disabilities.

The positional nature of a legal position is particularly evident if we consider freedom as introduced by Robert Lee Hale (see Chapter 1). For Hale, it is always a question of liberty against liberty: exercising one's freedom necessarily entails limiting someone else's freedom, as in a zero-sum game. This idea relies on the idea that each person exerts some degree of coercion over other people's liberty, while their own liberty is subject to some degree of coercion by others. In other words, each freedom implies at least one "coercer" and at least one "coerce," or better, at least one party consuming a positive level of freedom – the coercer – and at least one other party consuming a corresponding negative level of freedom – the coercee. One consequence that resembles Hohfeld–Commons's scheme is that the coercer can consume freedom only if there is a correlative coercee. According to Hale, the economy thus has a structure of zero-sum legal positions: an increase of freedom for one party (the coercer) is related to a decrease of freedom for another party (the coercee).

3.2.   Positional goods: a primer

In a famous passage from Plutarch, Julius Caesar, upon passing by a small village of barbarians, asserted that "[f]or my part, I had rather be the *first man* among these fellows than the *second man* in Rome." In this assertion, Caesar confessed his willingness to renounce the larger and better private and public goods that he could consume in Rome (e.g., *panem et circenses*) to be in the position of *the first man* (a positional good) in a relatively poor community. Although Caesar solved the dilemma between positional and public or private goods by becoming the first man in Rome, this dilemma is at the basis of an huge number of choices for individuals (e.g., Frank 1985). Individuals prefer to be the first in a reference group, even if it is a second-rate reference group (e.g., a barbarian village) – this also holds for angels like Satan: in John Milton's *Paradise Lost*, Satan stated that it is "[b]etter to *reign* in Hell than *serve* in Heaven" (italics added). The experimental literature corroborates such a positions-matter argument (e.g., Solnick and Hemenway 1998, 2005). Similarly, Hopkins and Kornienko (2004) hypothesize that "it is not just that the car is big [enough for needs] but that it is bigger than those owned by the neighbors that also matters" (Hopkins and Kornienko 2004:1087–1088). That is, the Jones family's choice of a new car will depend not only on whether it is big enough for their family's own needs but also (if possible) on whether it is bigger than that of the Jones family's neighbours. Carlsson *et al.* (2007) tested this size-matters hypothesis through an experiment and found that people prefer bigger cars than the average size in their society.

As originally noted by Veblen (1899), each individual has the desire to "keep up with the Joneses" and therefore compares their position with the position(s) of other individual(s) when they choose their consumption. The literature refers to this type of consumption as the consumption of positional goods. Positional concerns are pervasive in numerous further socioeconomic domains (see Solnick and Hemenway 2005), such as income (Duesenberry 1949; Easterlin 1974), poverty (Sen 1983), employment (Neumark and Postlewaite 1993; Pagano and Vatiero 2019) and environment (Carlsson *et al.* 2010). In addition, the idea of a positional good has also been developed in the fields of sociology, psychology, anthropology and philosophy (cf. McAdams 1992; Sunstein and Ullman-Margalit 2001). Finally, positional goods play a pivotal role in people's happiness (e.g., Clark *et al.* 2008).

The main characteristic of the consumption of positional goods is that it is based on social scarcity, as distinguished by the consumption under physical scarcity. Consider once again the Jones family's choice of a new car: a car is physically scarce in the sense that the factors involved in the production of a car are scarce (e.g., materials), but the car is (also) *socially* scarce in the sense that the biggest car in a certain reference group is defined in relation to the bigness (or smallness) of neighbours' cars and to the fact that, by definition, *only one* car can be the biggest or the smallest. Karl Polanyi advances a similar distinction:

> [Physical or natural] scarcity reflects either the niggardliness of nature or the burden of the labor that production entails. But the highest honors and the rarest distinctions are few for neither of these two reasons. They are scarce for the obvious reason that there is no standing room at the top of the pyramid. . . . They would not be what they are if they were attainable to many. . . . Scarcity derives from the *non-economic order of* things.
>
> (Polanyi 1968:94, italics added)

Because of social scarcity, the consumption of positional good is thus defined as a zero-sum game: *if you go up, I come down* (see also Pagano 1999; Hopkins and Kornienko 2004). In a similar way, Hohfeld–Commons's scheme and Hale's freedom also have a structure of zero-sum – what one party gains, the other loses (cf. also Vatiero 2013).

Consider a simple analytical framework with two agents, $R1$ and $F1$, and denote with x, y and z three "pure" kinds of good: respectively, private, public and positional goods. Let us indicate with a capital letter the total quantity of every pure kind of good.[1] Following the analytical formulation of Gravelle and Rees (1981:516–517), we have in the case of the private good:

$$x_{R1} + x_{F1} = X$$

On the other hand, in the case of the non-optional public good,[2] we have:

$$Y_{R1} = Y_{F1} = Y \qquad\qquad [3.1]$$

Finally, in the case of positional goods, the total consumption is null. If $R1$ is the individual who has a positive consumption of a positional good, then $F1$ must have a negative consumption. In analytical terms, the total consumption is as follows:

$$z_{R1} + \left(-z_{F1}\right) = 0 \qquad\qquad [3.2]$$

Note that according to [3.1], if agent $R1$ consumes an additional quantity of a (non-optional) public good, then agent $F1$ has to consume an additional positive amount. Samuelson (1954:389) refers to that circumstance in terms of the *jointness of demand* or jointness in the consumption of (non-optional) public goods. A similar circumstance is in the case of positional goods: according to [3.2], if agent $R1$ consumes an additional quantity of a positional good, then agent $F1$ has to consume an additional negative amount. The only difference is in the sign of this *joint* consumption: negative for positional goods and positive for public goods. Also, the fact that the total consumption of a positional good is null (as in [3.2]) does not imply that production costs are null. For instance, in the case of the Jones family's choice of a new car, the production of cars would be costly, but the total amount of consumption of the positional good (to be the holder of the bigger or smaller car) is still null.

In a Cartesian plane with consumption for Robinson on the abscissa and consumption for Friday on the ordinates, as in Figure 3.1, we can

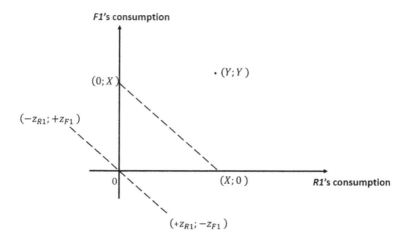

Figure 3.1 Consumption of private, public and positional goods.

illustrate the characteristics of the consumption of these three kinds of goods. In the case of private goods, given a certain total amount, other individuals consume a zero amount of what each individual chooses to consume. The consumption of private goods is thus represented by the segment $(X; 0)$ $(0; X)$ in Figure 3.1. For a public good, instead, each agent consumes the same positive amount as the other agent consumes. This is illustrated by the point $(Y; Y)$. Finally, a positional good is illustrated by the line $(-z_{R1}; +z_{F1})$ $(+z_{R1}; -z_{F1})$ for which the total amount of consumption is a zero-sum game.

In this (micro)economy characterized by three kinds of goods (private, public and positional goods) and two agents, R1 and F1, a positional good is included in the utility function f (twice differentiable), just like other economic goods. The utility functions for our two agents are then $f_{R1}(x_{R1}, Y, \pm z)$ and $f_{F1}(x_{F1}, Y, \mp z)$. Let us denote with MRS the marginal rates of substitution of agents and assume that the marginal cost of production of the good is equal to its price (this is the standard assumption of a context with transactors who are price takers). The optimality condition for a public good (cf. Gravelle and Rees 1981:517) – the Samuelsonian formulas – is as follows:

$$MRS(+y_{R1}) + MRS(+y_{F1}) = p^y \tag{3.3}$$

For a private good (cf. Gravelle and Rees 1981:517) the optimality condition is as follows:

$$MRS(+x_{R1}) = MRS(+x_{F1}) = p^x \tag{3.4}$$

Because of the jointness of demand/consumption, the optimality condition of positional goods follows the Samuelsonian formula:

$$MRS(+z_{R1}) + MRS(-z_{F1}) = p^z$$

Note that because the individual utility stems from individual preferences regarding consumption, one can imagine, as an extreme, that an individual may actually benefit from the negative consumption of a positional good, such as one with masochistic preferences who may revel in being the last, the poorest, the ugliest and so on. However, except for such extreme cases, one can assume that a positive level of the consumption of the good brings a positive utility, while a negative level of the consumption brings about a negative utility; in other words, the utility of a pure positional good depends negatively on the utility of the others. If Robinson is consuming a positive amount of positional good, then he has a positive utility; instead, Friday is consuming a negative amount and has a negative utility, which implies that

$MRS\left(-z_{F1}\right) < 0$. In formulas, the optimality condition can be rewritten as the following:

$$MRS\left(+z_{R1}\right) - \left\|MRS\left(-z_{F1}\right)\right\| = p^{z} \qquad [3.5]$$

One can observe that while in the case of the public good the efficiency condition involves a summation of marginal rates of substitution [3.3] and in the case of the private good it involves the equality of marginal rates of substitution [3.4], in the case of the positional good the efficiency condition involves the difference of marginal rates of substitution [3.5]. Following the diagrammatic exposition of Samuelson (1955), the total demand for a public good is the vertical addition of individual marginal valuations, and the total demand for a private good is the horizontal addition. Instead, in the case of a positional good, the total demand is given by the vertical subtraction of individual marginal rate curves: $MRS\left(+z_{R1}\right) - MRS\left(-z_{F1}\right)\|$. Therefore, the optimal quantity of a positional good is given by the intercept of the marginal cost curve and the vertical *subtraction* curve of marginal rates of substitution.

Finally, comparing [3.4] with [3.5], we note that for efficiency, Robinson should pay not only the marginal cost of production or price (as in the case of private goods [3.4]), but also the "costs" of Friday's negative consumption. Pareto-efficiency for positional goods implies that the price involves marginal cost p^{z} plus the *price* of negative effects on those who do consume a negative amount of the positional goods, $MRS\left(-z_{F1}\right)$. Namely, the price should be a sort of "double price" (cf. also Pagano 1999). Second, suppose that the market fails in guaranteeing optimal conditions, namely that each individual chooses on the basis of the price and not the external effects on others. In the case of public good, the good will be under-provisioned (cf. [3.3]), but in the case of positional good, one would observe an over-provision, because Robinson will neglect the costs for Friday (cf. [3.5]; see also Pagano 1999).

To better explain the differences among the consumptions of private goods, public goods and positional goods, let me label the positive difference between Robinson's marginal valuation and the price of a good as surplus or sur-*plus*. In the case of positional good, the surplus is given by the following:

$$Sur - plus = MRS\left(+z_{R1}\right) - p^{z}$$

And call surminus or sur-*minus* the disutility deriving from the negative consumption of a positional good for Friday, namely

$$Sur - minus = MRS\left(-z_{F1}\right)$$

People "consume more" positional goods not only for being the first and therefore for obtaining the surplus but also for not being the last in a ranking and, consequently, for not suffering the surminus. Hence, in the case of positional goods, agents are rivals for *both* surplus *and* surminus: they try to obtain the surplus *and* to avoid the surminus. In contrast, there is no surminus in the case of public goods (both agents have surplus) or private goods (Friday will consume a null level of the good consumed by Robinson). For this reason, there is "more rivalry" in the consumption of positional goods than in the consumption of private goods (and, consequently, than in the consumption of public goods). This higher level of rivalry can be considered a "double-rivalry," because the agents are rival for both the surplus and the surminus related to the consumption of positional goods. Also in terms of excludability, positional goods have different characteristics than do private and public goods. In the case of positional goods, excludability must include *both* the exclusion from surplus *and* the exclusion from surminus; in contrast, in the cases of private and public good, there is no Friday's surminus resulting from Robinson's positive consumption of the good. For this reason, positional goods have more excludability than do private goods, and consequently, one can delineate the condition of "double-excludability."

Figure 3.2 summarizes the characteristics of consumption for the triad of economic goods. Positional good is then defined as a double rival and double excludable good in the consumption. The novelty of this definition is that it takes into account the surminus coming from the consumption of the positional good. The surminus is quite neglected in the theoretical and empirical literature. One exception is Luttmer (2005), who investigates whether individuals feel worse off when others around them earn more. He finds that increases in neighbours' earnings reduce one's own happiness (namely, raise the level of surminus). Hence, it is not sufficient to focus the

	non-rivalry	rivalry	double-rivalry
non-excludability	PUBLIC GOOD		
excludability		PRIVATE GOOD	
double-excludability			POSITIONAL GOOD

Figure 3.2 A taxonomy of goods.

analysis only on the utility derived from consuming (a positive amount of) positional goods (e.g., the benefits from being the richer, the dominus, the owner of the biggest car, etc.) – which here it is called the surplus. Indeed, the condition of joint demand/consumption implies that there is also a negative effect (disutility or surminus) for the other agent who is consuming negative amounts of positional goods, such as the costs of being the poorer, the servus, the owner of the smallest car, etc.

3.3. Freedom as a positional good

Positional goods depend on social scarcity. Similarly, legal positions (claims, duties, powers, etc.) are socially scarce because their consumption cannot be universal; if one agent consumes a claim, at least one other has to consume a duty, by definition. In a similar way, volitional freedom is socially scarce for Hale. Unlike Mill (see page 10), for Hale each person exerts some degree of coercion over other people's liberty, while their own liberty is subject to some degree of control and coercion by others. The coercer can thus consume freedom only if coercion exists, and both parties cannot consume the same level of freedom, because the total consumption of Halean freedom (as well as the total consumption of each positional good) is by definition null (cf. also Fried 1998:51–54). There is, in other words, an idea of freedom as mutual coercion (i.e., that exercising one's own freedom necessarily entails limiting someone else's freedom) that overlaps with the zero-sum characterization of positional goods.

One consequence is that if legal positions are the same as positional goods, then the definition of rights involves positional concerns and costs. To demonstrate this thesis, let's consider Defoe's story of Robinson Crusoe; the example is from Vatiero (2013). Before the arrival of Man Friday $F1$, Robinson Crusoe $R1$ reached his physical limits: he spent his resources (e.g., time) in facing natural limits. When Friday arrives, social limits emerge, and Robinson starts to consume positional goods such as *power* (cf. Pagano 1999) and Halean volitional freedom, given that each of his choices also depends on Friday's choices, and vice versa.

On the island, Robinson and Friday can consume public goods, private goods and positional goods. For instance, the liquor recovered from the boat can represent a private good, whereas the air of the island exemplifies a public good. Finally, a Halean volitional freedom may be the freedom from naked people. Defoe describes Robinson as annoyed because Friday walks around naked. This freedom is investigated as a positional good and indicated by z. Assume the private good as numeraire, for instance a certain quantity, say a sip, of liquor. The marginal rate of substitution indicated with $MRS(z)$ stands for how many sips of liquor Robinson is willing to give up and Friday is willing to accept to, respectively, "acquire" and "sell" freedom from people walking naked. The marginal social value of a variation of freedom Δz is given by

$$MRS_{R_1}\left(+\Delta z\right) + MRS_{F_1}\left(-\Delta z\right)$$

Finally, let us denote the marginal cost of the variation of freedom in terms of the numeraire as $c(\Delta z)$. Indeed, freedom is costly; for instance, it calls for the "production" of specific conditions. On Robinson's island, it means, for instance, the production of new clothes for Friday. In the modern economy, it would signify the "production" of structures for enforcing freedoms (e.g., courts, patrols and so on). Therefore, the first-order condition for the "socially" optimal quantity of freedom can be written (cf. [3.5]) as

$$MRS_{R_1}\left(+\Delta z\right) - ||\, MRS_{F_1}\left(-\Delta z\right)\, || = c\left(\Delta z\right) \qquad [3.6]$$

In [3.6], the difference between individual marginal valuations is thus set equal to the marginal cost. Note again that condition [3.6] is different from the standard optimality condition for private goods, where all marginal valuations of substitution between private goods are equal to the respective marginal costs. That is, from a diagrammatic view, individual demand should be derived vertically for positional goods (and not horizontally, as in the case of private goods).

Let us place the relative price (the price of freedom in terms of sips of liquor) on the Y axis and Robinson's volitional freedom on the X axis, as in Figure 3.3; to take into account positional concerns, Robinson should not only pay a price for the marginal cost of freedom, $c(\Delta z)$, but also pay a price for the relatively "dangerous" effect on Friday $||\, MRS_{F_1}\left(-\Delta z\right)\, ||$. The price should thus be a sort of a "double price": in our case, it is determined by the price of new clothes for Friday plus the price for remunerating Friday for selling his freedom to walk around naked.

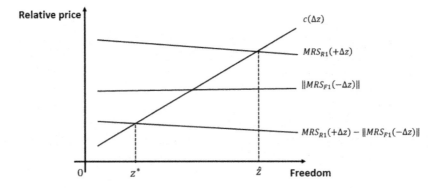

Figure 3.3 Freedom and vertical subtraction rule.

In terms of efficiency, the positional nature of freedom and legal positions may and does lead to Pareto-inefficient equilibrium. Indeed, if agent $R1$ considers only the marginal cost $c(\Delta z)$ as in the case of private goods, he will choose a level of freedom equals to $\hat{z}$, while the level which takes into account the effect of freedom over agent $F1$ is lower: it is the level z^*.

Once legal positions are represented as positional goods, the allocation of legal positions (as the allocation of each positional good), should therefore also consider costs of servus, namely of parties who consume a negative amount of legal position. When the market fails in guaranteeing optimal conditions, an individual chooses considering only production costs but not external effects on others and will neglect the costs for servus. It is therefore not sufficient to focus the analysis only on the utility derived from consuming (a positive amount of) legal positions – such as the benefits from having claims, powers, etc.; the positional nature of legal positions implies that there is also a negative effect (disutility or surminus) for the other agent, who is consuming a negative amount of legal positions (e.g., the costs of duty, liability, etc.).

3.4. The inevitable costs of defining rights

According to the contributions of Hohfeld, Commons and Hale, each legal position correlates with an adverse legal position. One consequence is that the freedom of one party can be increased by restrictions provided through the law on the freedom of others:

> Each person exerts some degree of coercion over other people's liberty, which at the same time his own liberty is subject to some degree of control by others. For the state to step in and suppress every liberty to restrict other people's liberty would indeed be oppressive. But it is a fallacy to assume that every attempt by the state to control and revise the economic results of bargaining involves a net curtailment of individual liberty.
>
> (Hale 1951:401)

Let us focus on the definition of property rights. In the Coase theorem, the definition of property rights yields to Pareto-efficiency (efficiency thesis), and the efficiency is attained independently from the initial allocation of property rights (invariant thesis). Nevertheless, if we consider the adversarial or positional nature of legal relations, the definition of rights, duties, powers, etc. creates positional concerns and *social costs*. Public official party should define rights and govern by law market failures and externalities, but such a definition of rights creates or redistributes legal positions that are characterized by positional concerns. Even market exchange in the economy, basing on property rights, is a legal structure of mutual coercion. The price states the conditions that permit consumption for one agent while restricting such consumption for another agent.

To better understand this issue, it is worthy also to mention the view of Oliver Wendell Holmes in his treatise *The Common Law*. He singled out competition as the primary instance of a peculiar situation, namely, when the law allowed someone to injure someone else's property, even intentionally, with impunity. So, for instance, an individual has a right to "establish himself in business where he foresees that the effect of his competition will be to diminish the custom of another shop-keeper, perhaps to the ruin of him" (Holmes 1881:144–145; see also Giocoli 2014). Holmes as well as Commons and Hale realized that each legal relationship, even in a competitive regime, is based on a degree of duress and, in particular, of coercion.

Consider also the example of the tradename. A public official will punish your use if you do not have the right to such a tradename or will punish others who make use of your tradename. This is to avoid the *common resources* problem and stimulate investments in innovation. On the other hand, according to Beebe (2010), the supply restrictions generated by intellectual property rights help preserve the distinct character of status symbols or positional goods (e.g., the Gucci logo on a handbag). Negative externalities are therefore borne by those who cannot afford such positional goods.

In similar terms, when referring to *intellectual monopoly capitalism*, Pagano (2019) notes that the advent of the knowledge economy has come together with a massive privatization of knowledge. Even if it has a non-rival nature, knowledge has been privatized since the 1980s and transformed into the intellectual monopolies of firms. Although intellectual property rights create incentives to invest in knowledge, Ugo Pagano emphasizes the negative effect that intellectual monopoly has on the intellectual investments of other firms. In terms of legal correlatives, a firm with IPR has a claim based on IPR enforced by a public official actor, whereas a firm without such rights has a duty enforced by a public official and/or a liability in this market.

More generally, no (property) right is a "free lunch" (see also Pagano 2012a; Pagano and Vatiero 2015). In the case of legal positions, the rule maker should take into account not only benefits deriving from defining an institutional arrangement that could improve efficiency (cf. the Coase theorem) but also the costs involved in that institutional arrangement, which is in turn characterized, owing to the adversarial nature of legal relations, by positional concerns. For such an adversarial or positional nature of legal positions, the definition of (property) rights by public official *P* is never neutral, as the Coase theorem instead suggests.

Notes

1 The description of positional goods in this chapter has at least two limits. First, each good could be characterized by features of private, public and positional goods. For instance, the car is a private good (a good for individual transportation), but the choice to purchase a car can lead to public and positional concerns: the use of a car produces

public bad or externalities (e.g., pollution, traffic, etc.), and the size of car can create positional concerns in order to be the individual with the bigger/biggest car (cf. Hopkins and Kornienko 2004). This chapter is limited, for the sake of simplicity, to an analysis of pure goods: either private, public or positional. Second, the simple model in this chapter focuses on a two-individuals case: one party consumes a positive level of positional goods, and a second party consumes a corresponding negative amount. This description therefore does not capture features of n-individual cases in which consumption of positional goods by individuals may be ranked and not only expressed as positive or negative.

2 Public goods can be optional and non-optional (cf. Gravelle and Rees 1981:516). In the first case, every agent *can choose* to consume any amount of the output produced, including zero: $Y \geq \gamma_{R1} \geq 0$ and $Y \geq \gamma_{F1} \geq 0$. The case of non-optional public goods is when each agent *has to* consume the total amount produced (cf. Gravelle and Rees 1981:516) – for instance, in the case of national defence against foreign countries, all inhabitants of the country have to consume the total quantity produced. Samuelson (1954:387) and (1955:350) refers specifically to the case of non-optional public goods.

4 The competitive dimension of transactions

Let us consider a familiar setting for transaction cost economics literature (cf. Hart 1995): a supplier of a widget who can invest in asset-specificity à la Williamson and a client (e.g., a car manufacturer) who buys this widget. For instance, this investment can represent a specific piece of equipment, bought by a supplier and needed for joint production with the car manufacturer. Or this investment can represent a relocation of a supplier's factory closer to the car manufacturer (e.g., the well-known Fisher Body–General Motors case). In both cases, note that the supplier's investment may increase revenues of both parties within the specific relationship. In an ideal world, the parties would write a state-contingent contract and rely on an external third party, a judicial system whose power comes from the political monopoly of power, to settle their conflicts ex post. To ensure an ex ante contracted outcome, the external third party will observe contracting parties' conduct and eventually impose penalties or other requirements if contracted obligations are not met. However, according to incomplete contract theory (e.g., Tirole 1999; Hart 2017), this external enforcement is costly. In the parlance of incomplete contract theory, the exact nature of the widget, though it is potentially observable by parties, is not verifiable by the external legal enforcer.

However, as this chapter underlines, the incompleteness of contracts is not sufficient to explain how holdup risk arises. The other condition that plays a pivotal role in the emergence of opportunistic behaviours is the ex ante asymmetry in the market: while the investor is locked in a relationship (namely there are no alternatives in the outside market), the non-investor has available alternatives. This diminishes the incentives for contracting parties to make specific investments and can encourage them to abandon the contractual form and manage the transaction with a different form – for instance, via a vertical integration in order to conduct the transaction within a single firm and save transaction costs (cf. Coase 1937). This chapter also shows that institutional arrangements aimed at alleviating the problems of holdup reduce or eliminate this asymmetry in the market.

4.1.   The role of the outside market in the emergence of holdup risk

The risk of holdup diminishes the incentive for investing. This is one of the main results of the incomplete contract theory. Denote the seller of a widget with R1 and the buyer with F1. For sake of simplicity, the assumption is that only seller R1 invests in asset specificity. For the nature of specific investments, when seller R1 has invested in asset specificity, he is locked in the specific relationship with F1, and it is therefore costly for investor R1 to switch to a potential, alternative buyer, such as F2. Conversely, if buyer F1 has not invested in the relationship, then he can move on alternatives, such as on seller R2, without costs (or at a relatively lower level of costs). This means that buyer F1 has reliable alternatives on the market (i.e., R2's widget), and therefore, F1 can credibly threaten to renegotiate the contract (holdup risk). The seller R1 will then disinvest in asset specificity.

In Figure 4.1, the dotted arrow between transactor F2 and transactor R1 indicates that, for the nature of specific investments, there are high costs for investor R1 in moving on F2, namely outside the specific relationship with F1. Instead, because agent R2 represents a reliable alternative counterparty for F1, the one-direction gray arrow from agent R2 through agent R1 indicates R2's effect (as a credible potential counterparty for F1) on R1's choice of investment. Moreover, the contracts are incomplete. It means that the external enforcement by the public official P is costly. The dotted arrows between the public official P and transactors denotes these enforcement costs. In the context of poor enforcement, the asymmetry of alternatives in the spot market renders credible threat of renegotiation after the investment in asset specificity. Under these conditions, the investor has reasons to underinvest. The transaction in this case is summed up in Figure 4.1.

Let's indicate with k the investment in asset specificity by agent R1. We denote with $C(k)$ and $c(k)$ the revenues of the investment k for agent R1,

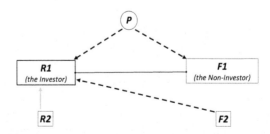

Figure 4.1 The role of alternatives in the outside market in the emergence of the holdup problem.

respectively in the specific relationship and in the spot market; because the investment for $R1$ is cost saving, the revenues $C(k)$ and $c(k)$ are in absolute value. Here, Hart (1995) makes three assumptions:

1 Specific investment k produces positive revenue within the relationship; that is, $\left\| \dfrac{dC(k)}{dk} \right\| > 0$.

2 Specific investment k also produces positive revenue for the alternatives in the outside market; that is, $\left\| \dfrac{dc(k)}{dk} \right\| > 0$. This effect for alternatives in the outside market is well-illustrated by Rajan and Zingales (1998:408).

3 The specific investment increases the revenue generated by the invest-ments as follows: $\left\| \dfrac{dC(k)}{dk} \right\| > \left\| \dfrac{dc(k)}{dk} \right\| > 0$.

While $R1$ invests in asset specificity, we assume that buyer $F1$ does not invest in asset specificity; that is, his revenue does not depend on his own investments. We denote with B a predefined contractual revenue if $R1$'s investment k is performed within the specific relationship and with b the revenues when $F1$ buys the widget in the outside market. If contracts are complete, then the specific relationship is secure, and the net surplus of relationship will be

$$\left[B - C(k) \right] - k$$

With complete contracts, all uses of resources will be specified in all possible eventualities and, therefore, observable by enforcing party P. For the threat of an ex post intervention of an enforcer, contracting parties are supposed to abide by their contracts. $R1$'s first-order condition in a context with complete contracts is thus given by the following:

$$\left\| \dfrac{dC(k)}{dk} \right\| = 1 \qquad\qquad [4.1]$$

In the case of incomplete contracts, transactors may instead breach the contract and switch to an on-the-spot market. The net surplus thus also involves revenues on the outside market, b and c, namely

$$\left[B - C(k) \right] - \left[b - c(k) \right] - k$$

Assuming that this rent is allocated according to a Nash-bargaining 50:50 sharing rule as in Hart (1995), under contractual incompleteness, $R1$'s first-order condition becomes the following:

$$\frac{1}{2}\left\|\frac{dC(k)}{dk}\right\| + \frac{1}{2}\left\|\frac{dc(k)}{dk}\right\| = 1 \qquad [4.2]$$

The comparison between first-order condition [4.1] and first-order condition [4.2] shows the standard result of the literature on holdups: the incompleteness of contracts reduces incentives to invest.

The problem depends on the asymmetry of the market rather than only on the incompleteness of contracts, however. The holdup risk is based on the fact that investment k determines different revenues for the investor within the relationship and outside of it. On the one hand, the investment within the specific transaction produces marginal returns at the level $\left\|\frac{dC(k)}{dk}\right\|$; on the other hand, the same investment, but outside the specific transaction, produces marginal returns at the level $\left\|\frac{dc(k)}{dk}\right\|$; and what is more important is that $\left\|\frac{dC(k)}{dk}\right\| > \left\|\frac{dc(k)}{dk}\right\|$. Instead, when the investment is general purpose (namely an investment which can produce the same return in both a specific transaction and in the outside market), condition [4.2] will be equal to the optimal condition [4.1].

Let's indicate with s the magnitude of safeguards for investments. Figure 4.2 (readapted from Williamson 1985a, 1985b) shows the contracting outcomes corresponding to different combinations of asset specificity k and institutional safeguards s. When the investment is general purpose, because the investor can resell their investment on the outside market in the case of opportunistic behaviours of counterparty without loss, there is no problem of underinvestments and therefore no need to define institutional safeguards. "Unassisted market" in Figure 4.2 represents the general-purpose technology ($k = 0$) supply relationship; in this circumstance, institutional safeguards are not needed (namely $s = 0$). "Opportunism" occurs instead when the contract

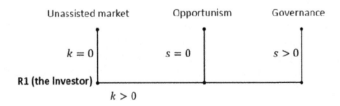

Figure 4.2 A scheme for specific investments and safeguards.

is supported by transaction-specific assets ($k > 0$) for which no safeguard is offered, viz. $s = 0$. This type of transaction is apt to be contractually unstable: it may imply the abandonment of specific investments or the introduction of "Governance" via contractual safeguards ($s > 0$) that would encourage the continued use of the $k > 0$ technology. Safeguards concerning governance could have several forms:

- The allocation of residual control rights à la Hart: "despite best efforts, non-standard contracting still experiences great governance strains, market contracting may eventually be supplanted by unified ownership (vertical integration)" (Williamson 1985b:185).
- Williamson's process of fundamental transformation: A further way to mitigate the holdup risk is to support trading regularities which signal intentions and commitment. This is the case for the process of fundamental transformation. With incomplete contracts characterized by specific investments, the ex ante competitive transaction is transformed ex post into a bilateral monopoly. In particular, "[t]ransactions that involve significant investments of a transaction-specific ($k > 0$) kind are ones for which the parties are effectively engaged in bilateral trade" (Williamson 1985b:187).

Hart's allocation of residual control rights and Williamson's fundamental transformation represent two remedies which, although both come from the same problem (of holdup) and alleviate the asymmetry in the market, work in different (and sometimes conflicting) ways, as we show later on.

4.2. Oliver Hart's assignment of residual control rights

In Hart's (1995) well-known analytical formulation, the two agents, $R1$ and $F1$, deal with a set of physical assets $A = \left(a_{R1}, a_{F1} \right)$. Agent $R1$, in combination with his asset a_{R1}, supplies the widget to agent $F1$. Agent $F1$, in combination with his asset a_{F1}, then uses this widget to produce output that is sold on the output market. From the perspective of Hart (1995), the assignment of residual control rights to the investor fosters investment. Residual control rights mean "the right to decide all usages of the asset in any way not inconsistent with a prior contract, custom, or law" (Hart 1995:30). That is, the allocation of residual control rights implies the specification of all uses that are missing in an incomplete contract. Accordingly, the economic benefit of the allocation of residual control rights is that the owner will receive a greater function of the ex post surplus created by a specific relationship. From this perspective, one can find a justification for vertical integration: if one wants to spur $R1$'s investments, then $R1$ has to have ownership over both assets, a_{R1} and a_{F1}. Note that after vertical integration, because the non-investor's physical assets are under the control (ownership) of the investor, it is not possible for the non-investor to switch to the outside market. This eliminates the credibility of a threat to move an on-the-spot market by the non-investor and therefore can safeguard the investments of the investor. Ownership thus matters in stimulating specific investments.

It is worth emphasizing that in Hart's model, revenues on the outside market, c, are positively correlated with ownership (see Hart 1995:37). That is, for agent $R1$,

$$\left\|\frac{dC\left(k;A^{R1}\right)}{dk}\right\| > \left\|\frac{dC\left(k;A^{R1}=\left\{a_{R1},a_{F1}\right\}\right)}{dk}\right\| \geq \left\|\frac{dC\left(k;A^{R1}=\left\{a_{R1}\right\}\right)}{dk}\right\|$$
$$\geq \left\|\frac{dC\left(k;A^{R1}=\left\{\varnothing\right\}\right)}{dk}\right\| \qquad [4.3]$$

Where A^{R1} indicates the set of assets owned by the seller (in our case, Robinson $R1$). Since the allocation of property rights over physical assets can affect the degree of investment, the holdup problem is transformed into the problem of *selecting the ownership structure*, which ensures second-best outcomes.[1]

Because alternatives in the outside market play a prominent role in the emergence of the holdup problem, it is not surprising that alternatives in the outside market play a role in mitigating the problem of holdup. Indeed, an ex ante context where non-investor $F1$'s alternatives in the outside market make his renegotiation with investor $R1$ credible is transformed by the assignment of residual control rights to $R1$ in an ex post context where non-investor $F1$ becomes a branch of $R1$ (vertical integration). One consequence is that non-investor $F1$ cannot threaten to switch on potential transactor $R2$. For this reason, $R1$'s choices of investment are no longer affected by potential transactor $R2$, and therefore, in Figure 4.3, there are no arrows (indicating an influence) between $R1$ and the outside market.

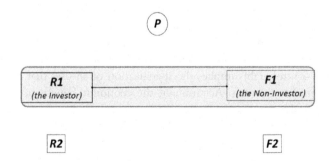

Figure 4.3 Alternatives in the outside market after the allocation of residual control rights.

Moreover, according to Margaret Blair and Lynn Stout, the manager in a public corporation (but it holds also for the entrepreneur in a firm) substitutes the public official in a transaction:

> to resolve disputes between parties for whom resolution through explicit contracting is too costly . . . or to settle an internal dispute over transfer prices between two units or subsidiaries of the same corporate, or between two individuals in a firm over work assignments, promotions, or division of a bonus pool.
>
> (Blair and Stout 1999:284–285)

For this reason, there is no arrow in Figure 4.3 between the public official and transactors.

4.3.   Oliver Williamson's fundamental transformation

According to Williamson, owning specific investments may instead have a commitment role, which makes it costly for the counterparty to move to alternatives in the outside market. Williamson argues that specific investments may reduce the field of available alternatives from a large number – that is, the ex ante bargaining situation – to a small number – that is, the ex post bidding bilateral monopoly – and that such a transformation should decrease the risk of opportunistic behaviours. Williamson describes this process by using the notion of fundamental transformation. Thanks to the parties' durable investments in transaction-specific assets, a market configuration characterized by large numbers bidding at the outset will be changed into an ex post market configuration characterized by a bilateral monopoly.

While specific investments are the origin of the problem of holdup in the standard literature, for Williamson own specific investments may mitigate holdup problems. Indeed, specific investment has a commitment role in the relationship that favours a continued bilateral trading relationship. For instance, if a firm acquires specialized assets (e.g., capital, knowledge or skills), that firm is better prepared than others for transactions. It means that it can be costly for the counterparty to exit or to threaten to exit (holdup): "Faceless contracting is thereby supplanted by contracting in which the pairwise identity of the parties matters" (Williamson 1985a:62).

This means that the specific investment, on the one hand, generates the conditions for investor's lock-in in the investor and, on the other hand, produces a credible commitment by determining the so-called transactional residual. In this respect, investments may affect the counterparties' alternatives in the outside market, and as a by-product, they may limit or prevent the counterparty's potential holdup.

The Williamsonian fundamental transformation might be related to the literature on the deterrence entry (e.g., Bain 1956; Sylos-Labini 1969; Spence 1977; Dixit 1980; Allen *et al.* 2000). According to this literature, sunk investments may be a tactical device adopted by incumbents to deter entry and raise rivals' costs. The incumbent, increasing the level of own sunk investments, may hurt profits of actual and potential competitors. Because investments will act as a signal of commitment to fierce competition, actual and potential competitors' choices will be significantly influenced by resulting ex post level of competition in the market.

By using the deterrence effect of non-contractible investment as an enforcement device for the incomplete contract, the incumbent may strategically decide to overinvest to prevent entry. That is, asset specificity may even constitute an endogenous enforcement device for incomplete contracts (cf. Nicita and Vatiero 2014). For instance, an overinvestment in asset specificity, under an incomplete contract framework, may create what Buehler and Schmultzer (2008) call an "intimidating effect" on prospective competitors – that is, an investment that, if observed before entry, may endogenously discourage the entry of new firms. Another example is the investment in capacity. It represents both the standard example of specific investments (cf. the General Motors–Fisher Body case) and a threat/commitment to a price war which may affect the choices of (new entrant) firms (see Dixit 1980). Specific investments in capacity can thus solve the holdup problem because such investments have a deterrent effect (Nicita and Vatiero 2014).

Let us offer an analytical representation. Using Bulow *et al.'s* (1985) terminology, investments are either strategic substitutes or strategic complements. One party's strategic substituting investment lowers their counterparty's market position, whereas one party's strategic complementary investment raises a counterparty's market position. We focus on the former. If the investment k of agent $R1$ is strategic substitute, this investment can affect the structure of the market, by making the transaction between $F1$ and his potential counterpart $R2$ more costly for agent $F1$; namely,

$$\frac{db(k)}{dk} < 0 \qquad\qquad [4.4]$$

Condition [4.4] means that agent $R1$ with his investment k can worsen the market position b of his counterparty $F1$. In so doing, condition [4.4] relaxes Hart's model assumption that the specific investment of one party does not affect a counterparty's alternatives $R2$, namely the assumption that $\dfrac{db(k)}{dk} = 0$. Indeed, except for effects of ownership in [4.3], alternatives in the outside market are exogenous in the Hart model.

Given these effects of investment on the alternative revenue in the outside market, the net surplus becomes

$$[B - C(k)] - [b(k) - c(k)] - k$$

And, $R1$'s first-order condition becomes (using a Nash-surplus-sharing rule):

$$\frac{1}{2}\left\|\frac{dC(k)}{dk}\right\| + \frac{1}{2}\left\|\frac{dc(k)}{dk}\right\| + \frac{1}{2}\left\|\frac{db(k)}{dk}\right\| = 1 \qquad [4.5]$$

Incentives in investments with "endogenous" alternatives in the outside market in [4.5] lead to a higher level of investments with respect to the case, assumed by Hart (1995), in [4.2]. The potential to affect counterparty alternatives in the outside market, namely $\dfrac{db(k)}{dk}$, provides $R1$ with a further incentive to invest in transaction-specific assets, beyond the potential coming from the specific relationship, i.e., $\dfrac{dC(k)}{dk}$, or from his alternatives in the outside market, i.e., $\dfrac{dc(k)}{dk}$.

In addition, note that the level of investments with endogenous alternatives in the outside market can be equal even to the efficient level as in [4.1]. Indeed, with endogenous alternatives in the outside market, investor $R1$ can overinvest or invest at the optimal level even if contracts are incomplete. Because the investments k of agent $R1$ might reduce the alternatives in the outside market of agent $F1$ with a marginal return such that $\left\|\dfrac{db(k)}{dk}\right\| > 0$, if

$$\left\|\frac{db(k)}{dk}\right\| \geq \left\|\frac{dC(k)}{dk}\right\| - \left\|\frac{dc(k)}{dk}\right\| \qquad [4.6],$$

the investor $R1$ has an incentive for investing which is equal to the first-best circumstance as in [4.1] or higher. The economic rationale for this kind of (over)investment is that under an incomplete contract, investments reduce a counterparty's credible threat to exit from the contract. (Over)investment acts as an endogenous and private enforcement device for supporting credible commitment in incomplete contracts. To rephrase, incentives that arise out of the fundamental transformation might compensate for, or even exceed, the reduction of incentives caused by incomplete contracts and holdup. Accordingly, parties may solve the problem of opportunism by implementing a certain market configuration – that is, a bilateral monopoly – rather than by agreeing to a certain contractual configuration. This means that transaction-specific assets might be self-enforceable even in a context with incomplete contracts. Investments in asset specificity under condition [4.6] may be sufficient to solve contractual failures deriving from investments in asset specificity.

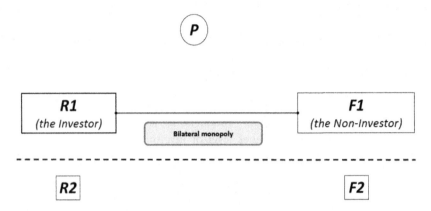

Figure 4.4 Bilateral monopoly as the result of fundamental transformation.

In summary, the specific investments of investor $R1$ may diminish non-investor $F1$'s alternatives in the outside market and, as a by-product, the credibility of the holdup threat by $F1$. In the case of a bilateral monopoly, non-investor $F1$'s opportunistic behaviour is extremely costly because there are no free alternatives to the specific relationship with investor $R1$. In an ex post market configuration resulting from fundamental transformation characterized by a bilateral monopoly (see Figure 4.4), the threat of opportunistic behaviour is not credible.

4.4. The "trade-off" between Hart and Williamson: a reappraisal of the General Motors–Fisher Body case

According to Hart, specific investments are the origin of the problem of the holdup, and the assignment of residual control rights is one of the remedies. Williamson, however, argues that specific investments may "transform" the configuration of alternatives in the outside market, and asset specificity in particular acts as an enforcement device against holdup. One consequence is that investors can invest at the optimal level or more (cf. [4.4], [4.5], [4.6] and related discussion) even with incomplete contracts. In other words, because each transaction among parties creates a transaction residual that favours a continued bilateral trading relationship, specific investments can mitigate the holdup phenomenon, even without the allocation of residual control rights. As noted by Williamson (1985a:62), "[t]his fundamental transformation has pervasive contracting consequences." One of these consequences is that there is no need for parties to design complex contracts which would further increase protection for investors against holdup, as the commitment effect of asset specificity ensures this protection against opportunism.

The assignment of residual control rights can therefore be unnecessary or even undesirable if it distorts the fundamental transformation process. Because market alternatives can change thanks to the allocation of residual control rights (see [4.3]), parties may have low to null incentives to invest in order to *still* transform such alternatives in the outside market. In other words, the solution à la Hart that changes a party's alternatives via residual control rights crowds out the solution à la Williamson, which changes a party's alternatives via specific investments.[2]

This framework can be useful to reassess the most extensively discussed textbook case study in economic literature on vertical integration due to a holdup (cf. Coase 2006): the case of General Motors and Fisher Body. In 1919, General Motors agreed to purchase metal car bodies exclusively from Fisher Body. Despite this, after the first few years of procuring the car bodies from Fisher Body, General Motors found that its demand for automobiles dramatically increased. Indeed, in the 1920s, the car market registered a huge and unforeseen rise in demand for closed car bodies, a demand that was unexpected by manufacturers such as Henry Ford, who said, "No one in his right mind would ride behind that much glass" (cf. Lamm 1978:n.a.). General Motors therefore encouraged Fisher Body to increase its capacity and, in particular, to build a factory near General Motors operations. Fisher Body, however, was concerned about the risk of holdup deriving from such specific investment (locating its plants near the General Motors assembly plants). The tension between General Motors and Fisher Body became *intolerable* (cf. also Crocker and Masten 1996), and by 1926, General Motors had acquired Fisher Body.

In contrast, the claim here is that such vertical integration depended on Fisher Body's strategy to increase its alternatives in the outside market and the vain attempt of General Motors to transform the market configuration. Indeed, there is a further part of the story which has to be narrated: General Motors required Fisher Body not only to build a new body plant near a General Motors assembly plant in Michigan (Flint) but also, as Coase (2000) adds, to close the Fisher Body plant in Detroit. Thanks to the skills of the Fisher brothers,[3] Fisher Body was able to fulfil the terms of the contract with General Motors (thus, an additional plant was not needed) and also to supply other automaker firms, such as Ford. Freeland (2000:40), in particular, stresses the relevance of the "desire [of General Motors] to prevent competitors from using Fishers' services" as one of the main factors inducing the complete acquisition:

> These fears were magnified in mid-1919, when Fisher obtained its largest order for closed [bodies] ever from Ford. Fearing that Ford was

experimenting with closed bodies on the inexpensive Model T, GM [i.e., General Motors] management worried that they were about to fall further behind their primary competitors in an important strategic area.

(Freeland 2000:41)

Moreover, between 1919 and 1926, Fisher Body also wanted to vertically integrate downstream or to vertically integrate with automakers (e.g., Ford and Studebaker).

There have been rumours for the past few years that the Fisher Body organization was intending to get into manufacture of the total car instead of just selling bodies to other car manufacturers. There were also persistent rumours that two other auto builders, Ford Motor Co. and Studebaker, have been attempting to buy out the Fisher brothers.

(Lamm 1978:n.a.)

In a simple scheme, as in Figure 4.5, the transaction before the 1926 merger included Fisher Body (denoted by FB), General Motors (denoted by GM) as well as competitors of General Motors (given that Fisher Body was able to supply closed bodies to them); however, it did not include Fisher Body's competitors because the exclusive deal with Fisher Body implied that General Motors could not buy from alternative sellers such as Wilson and Briggs. While Fisher Body wanted to continue to sell its closed bodies at a competitive price to competitors of General Motors and "it would have been less costly to supply them from Detroit rather than from Flint" (Coase 2000:29), General Motors wanted to "transform" the initial market configuration in a bilateral monopoly, by closing Fisher Body's plant in Detroit. Moreover, there were rumours that Fisher Body wanted to move downstream or integrate with competitors of General Motors: Ford or Studebaker.

After the 100% acquisition, transactions between Fisher Body and competitors of General Motors were nulled (as was the possibility that Fisher Body would move downstream). The Fisher Body–General Motors merger dramatically changed the transaction configuration. It transformed not only

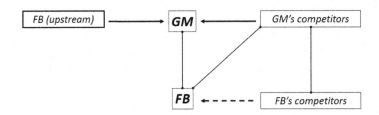

Figure 4.5 FB–GM's transaction before 1926.

the relationship between General Motors and Fisher Body (which became a General Motors branch) but also the conditions of competition in the market. According to Freeland (2000), after the acquisition of Fisher Body, competitors of General Motors, lacking access to products of Fisher Body, had a significant reduction in returns, whereas General Motors greatly increased its output: "The purchase of Fisher thus had a dramatic impact on [General Motors'] position, providing at least a temporary advantage over its major competitors" (Freeland 2000:56).

On the one hand, vertical integration could have enhanced the relationship, threatened by hold-up risk, between Fisher Body and General Motors as Hart suggests; on the other hand, it is likely that it reduced the competition downstream (and upstream) and incentives for investing (à la Williamson) in the alternatives in the outside market.

4.5.   The road ahead: reconciling Hart with Williamson

The Fisher Body–General Motors story shows that, even admitting that it improved the specific relationship between Fisher Body and General Motors, it is likely that vertical integration reduced the competition downstream (and upstream). This potential trade-off between incentives in the specific relationships and outside is particularly relevant for antitrust implications concerning contractual remedies (e.g., exclusive dealings) or mergers, which tend to diminish incentives deriving from market competition.

Intriguingly, Oliver Hart writes,

> I have supposed that any contract [agents] enter into, including a change in ownership, has a negligible impact on any other parties. . . . In practice, of course, *not all integration decisions are made for efficiency reasons.* Firms integrate vertically *to foreclose on rival purchasers and suppliers.* The theory developed in this book should be a useful ingredient in future work in this area.
>
> (Hart 1995:55, fn. 36, italics added)

This chapter considers endogenous outside options via specific investments and thus represents an extension of Hart (1995). With the Williamsonian process of fundamental transformation in mind, specific investments can be aimed at transforming market configuration. For instance, Fisher Body invested in capacity to also furnish competitors of General Motors with Fisher Body's closed metal bodies. In theory, General Motors might also make a similar investment: General Motors might invest to increase its potential counterparties; for instance, General Motors "may decide to develop a car that can use bodies produced by a number of different suppliers, rather than only [Fisher Body]" (Hart 1995:27). Then, Hart hypothesizes that one investor can strategically determine the degree of specific investment in order to change ex post competition; but this insight is not developed in the Grossman–Hart–Moore model.

Here, I report several results of this chapter. First, asset specificity may be able to preserve or increase, rather than decrease, the investor's ex post bargaining power. Second, due to its impact on the outside market, the specific investment might reduce the risk of holdup, namely the potential to switch to alternatives. Third, because a process such as fundamental transformation can mitigate holdup risk, it renders unnecessary (or even potentially undesirable) the allocation of Hartian residual control rights. Indeed, if the protection of investments comes from an institutional arrangement (i.e., residual control rights), then parties have a lower level of incentive to invest in order to signal their commitment and/or transform the transaction, as in the fundamental transformation. This potential trade-off between the allocation of residual control rights and the process of fundamental transformation should be analysed when selecting the optimal ownership structure.

More generally, the analysis of a transaction in an incomplete contract context allows us to investigate the nexus among the definition and enforcement of rights, market structures, market strategies and incentives to invest. This shows, once again, the great versatility of transactional economics.

Notes

1 Indeed, while it encourages owner's incentives, the assignment of residual control rights will decrease non-owners' incentives to invest (cf. Hart 1995). Then, only second-best outcomes are possible.
2 This finding relates to the contribution of Rajan and Zingales (1998), in which authors identified a mechanism to allocate power – the access to a critical resource – which is alternative to the ownership mechanism of the Grossman–Hart–Moore model. This new mechanism is introduced because ownership may reduce alternatives in the outside market for the investing party in asset specificity – this effect is, using the words of Rajan and Zingales, "the dark side of ownership" (Rajan and Zingales 1998:390; cf. also pp. 460 ff.).
3 Michael Lamm (1978) writes that

> the manufacturing techniques pioneered by the Fishers included precision woodworking on a mass-production scale. Wooden components would interchange from one body to another and no longer had to be hand-fitted, as in carriage making. Fisher also pioneered sheet-metal stamping in a very crude but effective way.
>
> (Lamm 1978:n.a.)

Moreover, Michael Lamm notes,

> Fisher Body flourished not only by the virtue of the people involved, but also because of . . . the staging: being in the right place at the right time. Detroit at the turn of the century happened to be a small city where everyone interested

in automobiles knew everyone else. The Fishers soon became acquainted with all the important industry pioneers – these movers and shakers whose automotive nameplates still survive today: Henry Ford, Walter Chrysler, Ransom E. Olds, the Dodge Brothers, Alfred P. Sloan, Jr., Henry Leland, Charlie Nash and others.

Lamm 1978:n.a.)

5 The political dimension of transactions

Transactions within a firm are characterized by orders and hierarchy, as Coase's idea of firm and Commons's concept of managerial transaction suggest. The structure of rights, duties and liabilities which govern transactions within a corporation and *corporate transactors* (especially, managers, shareholders and workers) comprise its corporate governance (cf. Aoki 2001a:11). In the corporate governance research, one of the main issues concerns: Which corporate transactors' interest has to be served (first)? Adolf Berle is often depicted as the original defender of the principle that today know as shareholder primacy. He asserted in a forceful language that

> all powers granted to a corporation or to the management of a corporation, or to any group within the corporation . . . are necessarily and at all times exercisable only for the ratable benefit of all the shareholders as their interest appears. That, in consequence, the *use* of the power is subject to equitable limitation when the power has been exercised to the detriment of such interest, and however correct the technical exercise of it may have been. That many of the rules nominally regulating certain specific uses of corporate powers are only outgrowths of this fundamental equitable limitation, and are consequently subjected to be modified, discarded, or strengthened, when necessary in order to achieve such benefit and protect such interest.
>
> (Berle 1931:1049, italics in original)

Merrick Dodd disagreed and countered that the corporation is "an economic institution which has a social service as well as a profit-making function" (Dodd, 1932:1147–1148). Dodd claimed that the corporation is a legal entity created by the state for public benefits and therefore the proper purpose of the corporation (and the proper goal of managers) was not confined to making money for shareholders. It also included more secure jobs for employees, better quality products for consumers, and greater contributions to the welfare of the community as a whole. In this respect,

Dodd believed managers would become a sort of civil servants for the social role of corporations that they administered. About 20 years later, Adolf Berle abandoned his previous position based on shareholder supremacy to switch on Dodd's stakeholder view:

> the writer [Berle] had a controversy with the late Professor Merrick E. Dodd, of Harvard Law School, the writer holding that corporate powers held in trust for shareholders, while Professor Dodd argued that these powers were held in trust for the entire community. The argument has been settled (at least for the time being) squarely in favour of Professor Dodd's contention.
>
> (Berle 1954:169)

The main common feature of these perspectives is that the corporation is depicted as a social/political construct. This view coming from Veblen's (1923) and developed also by Berle and Means's (1932) seminal works and in the contributions of Mark Roe (e.g., Roe 2019, which concerns short-termism) shows that transactions within corporations are characterized by a political dimension. In the words of Berle and Means,

> Corporations are essentially *political constructs*. Their perpetual life, their capacity to accumulate tens of billions of assets, and to draw profit from their production and their sales, has made them part of the service of supply of the United States. Informally they are an *adjunct of the state itself.*
>
> (Berle and Means 1932:xxxviii, italics added)

This chapter shows that corporate governance and therefore transactional outcomes within the firm depend on polity. Corporate governance arrangements inside the firm between the corporate transactors (in particular, managers, shareholders and workers) of the big corporations interact strongly with a nation's politics. Nations, as a matter of polity and politics, may follow the interests of workers, of incumbents in a market or of certain innovative sectors; and, through institutional complementarity (see Milgrom and Roberts 1990; Aoki 2001b; Pagano and Vatiero 2015), multiple *corporate governance equilibria* may emerge.

According to institutional complementarity theory,[1] the choices in one domain (e.g., in the labour domain) act as exogenous parameters in other institutional domains (e.g., shareholder protections, market competition and innovation). In this setting, "one type of institution rather than another becomes viable in one domain, when a fitting institution is present in another domain and vice versa" (Aoki 2001b:225). The term "fitting" used by Masahiko Aoki invokes an evolutionary approach to institutional contexts. Indeed, this chapter explains the *diversity* (in the Darwinian sense[2]) of corporate governance regimes, especially of blockholding phenomena, around the world and over time, as the result of *political* or public choices in three complementary domains: labour protection, market competition and innovation.

5.1. The political argument over corporate governance

In a series of articles, Shleifer and his coauthors (e.g., La Porta *et al.* 1997, 1998, 1999, 2000, 2008; the so-called legal origin theory) claim that the diversity of corporate governance structures depends on the distinction between legal families, the common law vs civil law systems, which had arisen in the twelfth and thirteenth centuries in England and France (Glaeser and Shleifer 2002:1193). Because France was less peaceful than England at that time, there was a greater need for protection and control of law enforcers by the state in France; consequently, France adopted a civil law system characterized by fact-finding by state-employed judges and, later, a reliance on codes rather than judicial discretion. In contrast, England developed a common law system that relied on fact-finding by juries, independent judges and judge-made law rather than strict codes (see Siems 2007). Thanks to Britain's colonies, this distinction extended around the world. According to the legal origin theory, current diversities in corporate governance structures depend on this medieval distinction between the French civil law (and its variants) and English common law (and its variants) systems.

One of the main merits of the legal origin theory is to stress how a politics-based variation (in particular, the role of judges in a community) has affected current corporate governance. As noted by Roe (2003, 2006), however, the polity in this argumentation exists only in the initial choice of the legal system in a given jurisdiction (common vs civil law) and no longer plays a role in shaping the actual content or use of law after the initial choice of systems. Many scholars are sceptical that the political variation illustrated by the legal origin theory is sufficient to explain the current diversity of corporate governance structures. There is not just one politics-based argument for the evolution of corporate governance and corporate ownership structures but rather a combination of many (e.g., Hansmann and Kraakman 2001; Rajan and Zingales 2003; Roe 2003, 2006; Pagano and Volpin 2005; Perotti and von Thadden 2006; Culpepper 2011; Pagano 2012b; Ciepley 2013; Roe and Vatiero 2018).[3]

Here, we develop a further explanation on the basis of institutional complementarity theory aimed at investigating the link between transaction/transactors in a corporation and polity. The principal actors inside corporations – shareholders, managers and employees – are also political actors with their own interests. Shareholders seek dividends; managers seek autonomy and prestige; and workers seek job stability and good wages. Each seeks rules that favour themselves in contested transactions within the firm. They are at the three vertices in the triangle in Figure 5.1, with each side of the triangle representing a potential coalition between two of these actors. Coalitions of corporate transactors acting for group interests may seek to obtain, via polity, both immediate results and enduring institutions that promote their own current interests and preferences (e.g., March 1962; Gourevitch and Shinn 2005). Corporate governance arrangements inside a firm among these three main corporate transactors interact deeply with a nation's politics through party systems, political institutions, the political orientations of governments and coalitions, ideologies and interest groups. Without a political economy analytics, one can neither fully understand the structure of the modern corporation nor account for international differences.

Many of the differences between corporate governance regimes in advanced industrial countries are determined by political choices concerning labour protection, product market conditions and technology. However, a simple map from politics to economics to corporate governance cannot be written, because causation is bidirectional, as the dotted arrows in Figure 5.1 illustrate.

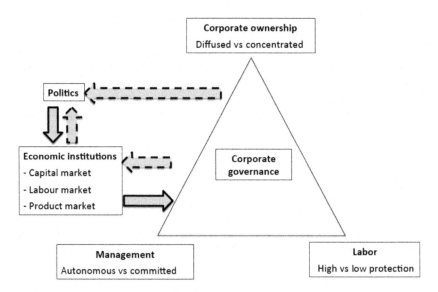

Figure 5.1 The "triangle" of political theory and corporate governance (readapted from Roe and Vatiero 2018).

In particular, corporate transactors contend for three types of rents:

1   corporate rents that concern surplus of the firm and its sharing between, for instance, shareholders and workers;
2   oligopolistic rents that are based on dysfunctional competition in the market of products;
3   technological rents that regard the division of returns from specific investments.

How a polity creates, supports or fights against these rents – namely how a polity decides to organize labour, market competition and innovation – can deeply affect the firm's corporate governance structures.

5.2.   The role of labour protection policies

The first complementarity that this chapter reports is that between the domain of corporate ownership and the domain of labour protection. It relies on corporate rents and specifically on how corporate surplus is shared between shareholders and workers. Countries characterized by stronger legal protection and voices for employees tend to have more-concentrated corporate ownership arrangements via their politics. So-called political reasons for the rise of labour protection abound. Among others, the middle class may prefer and vote for pro-labour policies and support a more corporatist system if it has relatively low financial savings and relatively high human capital (Perotti and von Thadden 2006). A second reason may be ideological: European social democracies pressured politics to give voice to the claims of workers in corporations (Roe 2003).

According to Mark Roe, countries characterized by stronger legal protections for employees (for some reason) tend to have more-concentrated corporate ownership arrangements:

> politics could, say, determine a particular labor structure, which might call forth only one type of ownership or management structure. For example, German codetermination – by which labor takes half of the board seats – demands concentrated ownership, because shareholders would do poorly if they failed to meet the boardroom's labor block with their block.
>
> (Roe 2003:5)

Put differently, shareholders may react to a higher participation of labour in the control of companies, by creating a higher concentration of corporate ownership in order to safeguard their rents. This dynamic suggests a causal relationship running from worker protection to corporate ownership arrangements. However, causation may run in the reverse direction as well: a certain degree of the concentration of owners' interests might easily encourage some sort of reaction from workers in terms of higher employment protection (cf. Aoki 2001b; Roe 2003; Ahlering and Deakin 2007; Gelter 2009; Belloc and Pagano 2013). In particular, the concentration of ownership in the capital market may urge employees to call for protection via politics:

> [E]arly in the twentieth century, the visible power of Germany's large banks, people's envy and resentment of rich industrialists, and the disorientation and anomie induced by Germany's rapid transformation from an agricultural nation into an industrial one helped to call forth codetermination to tame the bankers and industrialists, and to give the workers a voice in the strange new industrial enterprises.
>
> (Roe 2003:112–113)

Figure 5.2 shows this complementarity between blockholding and workers' voices. Two equilibria arise: one with a low level of both employment

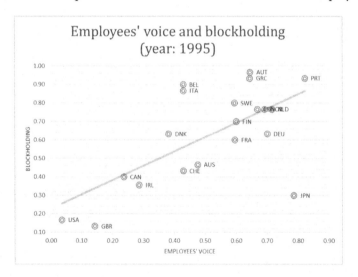

Figure 5.2 The complementarity between labour protection (as worker voices) and corporate ownership diffusion.

Notes: $y = 0.7749x + 0.227$; R-square = 0.41676; p-value < 1%.

Twenty developed countries: Australia (AUS), Austria (AUT), Belgium (BEL), Canada (CAN), Denmark (DNK), France (FRA), Finland (FIN), Germany (DEU), Great Britain (GBR), Greece (GRC), Ireland (IRL), Italy (ITA), Japan (JPN), the Netherlands (NLD), Norway (NOR), Portugal (PRT), Spain (ESP), Sweden (SWE), Switzerland (CHE) and the United States (USA).

Source: Data on blockholding is from La Porta *et al.* (1999); it includes 30 big corporations at the end of 1995, specifically the 20 largest firms and 10 firms with a market capitalization of at least $500 million in common equity for each country. The blockholder is defined as a corporate actor with 20% of voting rights. Data on employee voices in 1995 is from the Centre for Business Research at the University of Cambridge.

protection and capital concentration, as in the Anglo-Saxon corporations, and one characterized by a high concentration of ownership and high employee protection, as in the Continental European firms (except for Switzerland, which, for certain political reasons, is characterized by corporations more similar to the Anglo-Saxon *species* of firms than to the Continental European species; see Vatiero 2017b).

5.3.   The role of competition policies

A second complementarity concerns oligopolistic rents. The hypothesis is that a higher concentration of corporate ownership relates to higher barriers to market entry and vice versa.

Stigler (1971) argues that incumbents can acquire regulations that create rents for themselves, since they typically face lower information and organization costs than do dispersed agents. Rephrasing Stigler's argument in the case of the blockholding phenomenon, for lower information, organization and lobbying costs, one should observe higher barriers to entry into markets with corporations controlled by blockholders than with corporations characterized by minority shareholders. In such a scenario, the blockholder is not only better able than a minority shareholder to minimize agency costs (managers vs shareholders) but also to affect rules and rule makers via politics.

Barriers to entry moreover create oligopolistic rents that increase the benefits of control and support blockholding. Indeed, the control of these rents should push shareholders to concentrate ownership since ownership is the first tool to control (Hart 1995). Another reason that oligopolistic rents encourage blockholding is that they provide firms with financial resources without accessing external capital markets (e.g., because of an underdeveloped financial system), which could prompt the dispersion of ownership. Blockholders may thus enjoy oligopolistic rents for financing and oppose the development of financial development and pro-competition policies (Rajan and Zingales 2003). Consequently, in a complementary relationship, a higher concentration of corporate ownership relates to higher barriers to entry in the market(s).

However, if blockholders are not powerful enough to affect polity, then they could rely on other incumbent groups such as organized workers. Economists have long acknowledged the potential role of labour unions as rent-seeking organizations; for example, Salinger (1984) and Rose (1987) provide evidence that unions share rents from oligopolistic markets. More generally, insiders at large enterprises – for example, blockholders and firm employees – generally align against outsiders. Since regulatory protectionism can create rents that workers and owners can share, blockholders bribe workers with pro-worker legislation so that they will comply with anti-competition legislation. Since human capital risk cannot be diversified, workers will furthermore be induced to exert political influence not only at the level of worker claims but also in their riskiness, by choosing policies against unstable contestable markets. As a result, blockholders and workers can create a transversal group (or distributional coalition in the terminology of Olson 1982) to increase barriers to entry, limit market forces and preserve rents from those outside their group. In this respect, rent seeking and risks can push workers, allied with blockholders, to call for barriers to the market entry of newcomers. This argument may strengthen the hypothesis that the blockholder phenomenon brings about highly regulated markets.

Two equilibria arise for institutional complementarities: an equilibrium, with low regulation and capital de-concentration, and a second equilibrium, characterized by a high regulation and concentration of ownership. Consistently, Figure 5.3 shows this complementarity between the blockholding phenomenon and market regulation.

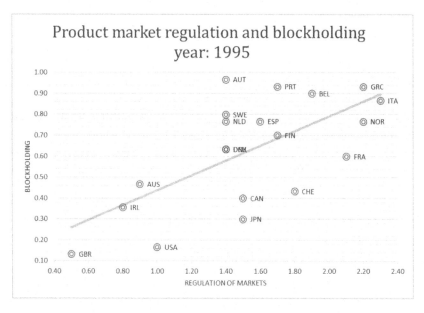

Figure 5.3 The complementarity between product market regulation and corporate ownership diffusion.

Note: $y = 0.3536x + 0.0834$; R-square = 0.4343; p-value < 1%.

Source: Data is from La Porta *et al.* (1999) for blockholding; data on the regulation of market in 1995 is from Nicoletti *et al.* (2000:79, Table A3.6).

5.4. The role of innovation policies

Mayer (2000), Hall and Soskice (2001) and Carlin and Mayer (2003) argue that a corporate governance equilibrium characterized by blockholding and strong employment protection supports activities with a modular stepwise progression and yields a production model with exceptionally high quality engineering and a low product-defect rate – both virtues associated with German and Japanese products. Instead, a corporate governance equilibrium with diffused shareholding and low employment protection benefits all-or-nothing innovation – for example, the granting of a patent for a new drug – thereby providing greater flexibility for work and for capital. Hall and Soskice (2001) distinguish incremental innovation based on small-scale improvements to existing products and production processes from radical innovation, which implies substantial shifts in production and the elaboration of completely new goods. The incremental innovation occurs primarily in sectors such as transport, mechanical elements, electrical machinery, civil engineering and chemical engineering, whereas radical innovation occurs in the information technology, pharmaceutical, chemistry and medical sectors.

In that respect, it is worth stressing that Hall and Soskice's (2001) argument also includes the asset specificity of investments, where the term "specificity" is along with Williamson's contributions (see Chapter 1). According to the authors, in an equilibrium with blockholding and strong employment protections, corporate actors "should be more willing to invest in specific and co-specific assets" (Hall and Soskice 2001:17), whereas in an equilibrium with diffused shareholding and weak employment protection, corporate actors "should invest more extensively in switchable assets" (Hall and Soskice 2001:17). This thinking derives from the fact that the former equilibrium provides "more institutional support for the strategic interactions required to realise the value of co-specific assets, whether in the form of industry-specific training, collaborative research and development, or the like" (Hall and Soskice 2001:17). Blockholding structures and strong labour protections should therefore stimulate incremental innovation and safeguard specific investments. However, there is also a reverse causation: owners and employees in incremental sectors all prefer political and corporate institutions that protect employees and encourage blockholding, each of which facilitates commitments to incremental technical improvement. By contrast, the actors within corporations in radical sectors largely prefer institutions that encourage limited commitments and flexible assets.

The specialization of a country is calculated as follows:

$$\frac{NoP \text{ in incremental sectors of the country}}{NoP \text{ in incremental sectors of all countries}} \Bigg/ \frac{NoP \text{ in all sectors of the country}}{NoP \text{ in all sectors of all countries}}$$

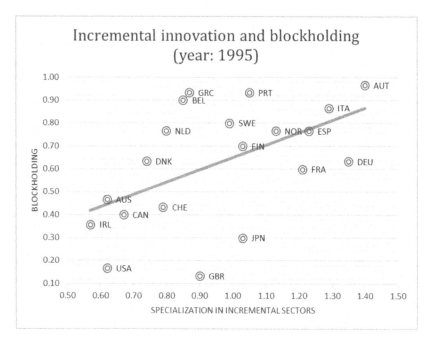

Figure 5.4 The complementarity between incremental innovation and blockholding.

Note: $y = 0.5392x + 0.1101$; R-square = 0.2798; p-value < 2%.

Source: Data on blockholding is from La Porta *et al.* (1999). Data on innovation concerning the number of patents (NoP) is from the database of the European Patent Office.

where the incremental sectors include transport, machinery and mechanical elements.

Two equilibria arise for institutional complementarities: one with radical innovation and capital de-concentration and a second one characterized by incremental innovation and a high concentration of corporate ownership. Figure 5.4 shows this complementarity between the blockholding phenomenon and innovation.

5.5.   Blockholding and politics

If economic rents are not "allocated" in advance by rules, there is ample space for corporate actors to exert pressures on regulatory, judiciary and political systems to grab a larger share of these rents. The argument here is that since the legal origin theory is insufficient to explain the phenomenon of blockholding in wealthy countries, the diversity of corporate governance regimes is affected by political or public choices in the domains of labour, market regulation and innovation policies. From that perspective, corporate ownership structures differ according to which institutional complements dominate, and consequently, the initial condition may have persistent lock-in effects. As a result, wealthy democracies have two broad packages: on the one hand, a first *corporate governance equilibrium* relates to competitive product markets, dispersed ownership, conservative policies for labour and radical innovative sectors; on the other hand, a second corporate equilibrium is characterized by relatively collusive product markets, concentrated ownership, pro-labour policies and incremental innovative sectors (cf. Franks and Mayer 1995; La Porta *et al.* 1999; Hall and Soskice 2001; Aguilera and Jackson 2003; Becht and De Long 2005; Gourevitch and Shinn 2005; Morck *et al.* 2005; Tirole 2006; Franks *et al.* 2009; Roe and Vatiero 2018). The elements in each package reinforce each other via politics, creating and supporting the diversity of corporate governance structures around the world and over time.

The proposed view also implies that the blockholding phenomenon may be weakened or strengthened if there are particular (political) conditions in complementary domains of labour, market regulation and innovation. For instance, Streeck (2011) argues that economic institutions in Germany have experienced a shift towards a decidedly pro-flexibility direction for the past two or three decades, in which industry-wide collective bargaining has declined and the bargaining system turned significantly more fragmented and pluralist. Similar processes have been observed in other countries, including Japan (Lechevalier 2014), France and Italy (cf. Amable 2015). The study of complementary domains might predict the evolution of these corporate governance regimes and any variation in their blockholding phenomena.

Notes

1 Complementarity is a recurrent and somewhat contentious topic. For instance, although Paul Samuelson in 1947 claimed that "the problem of complementarity has received more attention than is merited by its intrinsic importance" (Samuelson 1947:183), he later corrected himself by asserting that "the time is ripe for a fresh, modern look at the concept of complementarity" (Samuelson 1974:1255).

2 Looking at diversities of corporations and their corporate governance structures around the world and over time would have intrigued Charles Darwin. Vatiero (2017a) proposes a parallel between the evolution of corporate governance and that of biological species.

3 In particular, legal origin theory builds the so-called antidirector rights index to measure how strongly the legal system favours minority shareholders over managers or dominant shareholders in the corporate decision-making process, including the process of voting (cf. Table 1 in La Porta *et al.* 1998). It shows that the concentration of shares in a large public company is negatively related to minority shareholder protections. The reason is that firms cope with the poor protection of minority shareholders by concentrating corporate ownership (i.e., blockholding). With poor minority shareholder protection, "ownership concentration becomes a substitute for legal protection,

because only large shareholders can hope to receive a return on their investment" (La Porta *et al.* 1998:1145).

Some scholars (e.g., Lele and Siems 2007; Spamann 2010:469) have nevertheless advanced doubts about the accuracy of La Porta *et al.*'s (1998) minority shareholder protection index for certain countries. "Corrected" indexes provide no evidence of significant differences of minority shareholder protections among developed countries. For instance, Spamann (2010) recodes the antidirector right index of La Porta *et al.* (1998), and the resulting index deviates substantially from the original; the correlation between the correct and original indexes is only 0.53, and 33 out of 46 countries had to be corrected. Moreover, these doubts are confirmed by a data set developed by a project of law and finance at the Centre for Business Research at the University of Cambridge (see www.cbr.cam.ac.uk/research/research-projects/completed-projects/law-finance-development/). The authors build a new, extended minority shareholder protection index for five countries (i.e., the UK, the US, Germany, France and India) and code the development of the law for more than three decades (1970–2005). Using that data set, Lele and Siems (2007) argue that no significant difference emerges in minority shareholder protections between blockholder countries such as France and Germany and dispersed ownership countries such as the UK and the US. In some cases, France and Germany have greater minority shareholder protections than the US. It suggests that the blockholder phenomenon does not derive (only or significantly) from poor minority shareholder protections.

Roe (2002) uses the proxy of premium for control and finds counterexamples to the legal origin theory. For instance, the block premium in a blockholder country such as Germany is similar to that in the US. As Roe (2002:261) attests, "if current control premiums were our only measure of the quality of corporate law, we would be driven to conclude that corporate law only weakly explained variation in ownership dispersion in the world's richest nations." As such, he argues, other institutional conditions – weak product market competition, an inability to use incentive compensation effectively because it would disrupt employment relationships within the firm, and a high level of social mistrust that impedes the professionalization of management – may contribute to concentrate or de-concentrate corporate ownership.

In that light, the link between dispersed shareholder ownership and stronger shareholder protection is too unclear, at least in developed countries. Even if the legal origin theory represents the dominant view of the phenomenon of blockholding, it is not sufficient to explain the differences in corporate ownership structure among advanced countries, where minority shareholder protections are similarly well developed.

6 Concluding remarks and one (just one, but remarkable) research proposal

According to Commons, Coase and other institutionalists, a transaction represents an *action* – including but not limited to an exchange – that *transfers* a control or ownership over something from a transactor to another transactor. This transfer comprises the actions of two actual transactors but also the actions expected by potential transactors (e.g., alternatives to two actual transactors) and the power of a public official actor. This idea of transaction, as described here, is able to analyse the allocation of resources – the focus of microeconomics – at the *microscope* but also to understand the consequences of a transactor' choices on others – the core of economic science – as a *telescope* (cf. page 8).

Each transaction consists of the three main dimensions: the legal, competitive and political dimensions. The legal dimension concerns the actions of a public official actor that affect the transaction and transactors' choices; the competitive dimension involves interactions between a transactor and other transactors that, in turn, affect their choices; and finally, the political dimension involves the actions of transactors aimed at affecting the rule maker and rule enforcer (typically via polity).

Chapter 2 introduced these three dimensions of a transaction. Chapter 3 considered the legal dimension and focused on the adversarial nature of legal positions, which brings about positional concerns in the definition and allocation of (property) rights. Chapter 4, which concerned the competitive dimension, described the role of the outside market in both helping the emergence of the holdup problem and its remedies. Chapter 5 examined transactions within firms, corporate governance and their relations with polity.

Many avenues of research could advance from this conception of transaction (cf. Vatiero 2018), but one seems to be the priority: the study of the meaning of costs in such a transaction, namely transaction costs. Despite being one of the most invoked explanatory variables for the study of institutions and pervasive in every field of theoretical and applied economics, there are different and sometimes conflicting interpretations of the notion of transaction costs (e.g., Calabresi 1968; Macneil 1978; Dahlman 1979; Williamson 1981, 1993; Demsetz 1993; Allen 2000). A theoretical consensus about what transaction costs are has still not to be seen (Williamson 1979; Veljanovski 1982; North 1990a; see also Pagano and Vatiero 2015). I believe that the root of the vagueness surrounding the notion of transaction costs can be attributed not to the meaning of cost (economists have a consolidated literature on that), but to the lack of a clear-cut definition of "transaction."

Despite denouncing that "the concept of transaction costs . . . is largely absent from current economic theory" (Coase 1988:6), even Coase contributed to the vagueness of the notion by providing only a list of potential costs of market transactions and provided no clear definition (see also Bertrand 2012). In 1937, he included among transaction costs "the cost of using the price mechanism . . . of discovering what the relevant prices are" (Coase 1937:390) and "[t]he costs of negotiating and concluding a separate contract for each exchange transaction which takes place on a market" (Coase 1937:390–391); in 1960, Coase enriched the list by explaining that

> to carry out a market transaction, it is necessary to discover who it is that one who wishes to deal with, to inform people that one wishes to deal and on what terms, to conduct negotiations leading up to a bargain, to draw up the contract to undertake the inspection needed to make sure that the terms of the contract are being observed, and so on. These operations are often extremely costly.
>
> (Coase 1960:15)

Moreover, in "The nature of the firm," Coase gave a scientific foundation to explain why firms become larger or smaller:

> a firm will tend to expand until the costs of organizing an extra transaction within the firm become equal to the cost of carrying out the same transaction by means of an exchange on the open market or the costs of organizing in another firm.
>
> (Coase 1937:395)

And as "in a moving equilibrium" (Coase 1937:405), "[a]t the margin, the costs of organizing within the firm will be equal either to the costs of organizing in another firm or to the costs involved in leaving the transaction to be 'organized' by the price mechanism" (Coase 1937:404). According to Coase (1937), a transaction can thus be organized via the market-price mechanism or within a firm by the orders of the entrepreneur, depending on the costs of these two types of institutional mechanisms: market *vs* firm.

This book was not about the concept of transaction costs, but such costs can be derived from our conceptualization of transaction. First, according to the argument developed in this book, there are costs that come from the positional nature of rights (see Chapter 3). Also, given the commitment role of specific investments, there are costs in allocating Hart's residual control rights, because these rights could be unnecessary or even undesirable (see Chapter 4). Finally, there are costs due to political dynamics (see Chapter 5). Future works should study these transaction costs theoretically and empirically, but first need the meaning of transaction to be identified. That first step was the chief objective of this book.

References

Acemoglu D. (2003), "Why not a political Coase theorem? Social conflict, commitment, and politics," *Journal of Comparative Economics*, 31:620–652.

Acemoglu D. and S. Johnson (2005), "Unbundling institutions," *Journal of Political Economy*, 113(5):949–995.

Acemoglu D. and J.A. Robinson (2012), *Why nations fail: The origins of power, prosperity and poverty*, New York: Crown.

Acemoglu D., S. Johnson, and J.A. Robinson (2001), "The colonial origins of comparative development: An empirical investigation," *American Economic Review*, 91:1369–1401.

Aguilera R.V. and G. Jackson (2003), "The cross-national diversity of corporate governance: Dimensions and determinants," *Academy of Management Review*, 28(3):447–465.

Ahlering B. and S. Deakin (2007), "Labor regulation, corporate governance, and legal origin: A case of institutional complementarity?," *Law & Society Review*, 41(4):865–908.

Allen B., R. Deneckere, T. Faith, and D. Kovenock (2000), "Capacity precommitment as a barrier to entry: A Bertrand-Edgeworth approach," *Economic Theory*, 15(3):501–530.

Allen D.W. (2000), "Transaction costs," in Bouckaert B. and G. De Geest (eds.), *Encyclopedia of law and economics*, vol. 1, Cheltenham: Edward Elgar, pp. 893–926.

Amable B. (2015), "Institutional complementarities in the dynamic comparative analysis of capitalism," *Journal of Institutional Economics*, 12(1):79–103.

Anderson E. and M. Bensaou (1999), "Buyer-supplier relations in industrial markets: When do buyers risk making idiosyncratic investments?," *Organizational Science*, 10:460–481.

Aoki M. (1984), *The co-operative game theory of the firm*, Oxford: Clarendon Press.

Aoki M. (2001a), *Information, corporate governance, and institutional diversity: Competitiveness in Japan, the USA, and the transitional economies*, Oxford: Oxford University Press.

Aoki M. (2001b), *Toward a comparative institutional analysis*, Cambridge: MIT Press.

Arruñada B. (2017), "Property as sequential exchange: The forgotten limits of private contract," *Journal of Institutional Economics*, 13(4):753–783.

Bain J.S. (1956), *Barriers to new competition*, Cambridge: Harvard University Press.

Barnard C.I. (1938), *The functions of the executive*, Cambridge: Harvard University Press.

Becht M. and J.B. De Long (2005), "Why has there been so little block holding in America?," in Morck R.K. (ed.), *A history of corporate governance around the world: Family business groups to professional managers*, Chicago: University of Chicago Press, pp. 613–666.

Beebe B. (2010), "Intellectual property law and the sumptuary code," *Harvard Law Review*, 123(4):809–889.

Bellantuono G. (2019), "Incentive systems in multi-tier global chains," work in progress, *on file with author.*

Belloc M. and U. Pagano (2013), "Politics-business co-evolution path: Workers' organization and capitalist concentration," *International Review of Law and Economics,* 33(1):23–36.

Bemis E.W. (1908), "The street railway settlement in Cleveland," *Quarterly Journal of Economics,* 22(4):543–575.

Berle A.A. (1931), "Corporate powers as powers in trust," *Harvard Law Review,* 44(7):1049–1074.

Berle A. A. (1954), *The twentieth (20th) century capitalist revolution,* New York: Harcourt.

Berle A.A. and G.C. Means (1932), *The modern corporation and private property,* New York: MacMillan.

Bertrand E. (2012), "A key to Coase's thought: The notion of cost: The notion of cost," work in progress, *on file with author.*

Biddle J.E. and W.J. Samuels (2007), "Introduction to the transaction edition," in Commons J.R. (ed.), *Legal foundations of capitalism,* Clifton: Augustus M. Kelley, pp. ix–xxxiii.

Bigoni M., S. Bortolotti, F. Parisi, and A. Porat (2014), *Unbundling efficient breach,* Chicago: Coase-Sandor Institute for Law & Economics Working Paper No. 695.

Blair M.M. and L.A. Stout (1999), "A team production theory of corporate law," *Virginia Law Review,* 85(2):247–328.

Bowles S. (2004), *Microeconomics: Behavior, institutions, and evolution,* Princeton: Princeton University Press.

Bromley D. (1989), *Economic interests and institutions: The conceptual foundations of public policy,* Oxford: Basil Blackwell.

Buehler S. and A. Schmultzer (2008), "Intimidating competitors: Endogenous vertical integration and downstream investment in successive oligopoly," *International Journal of Industrial Organization,* 26(1):247–265.

Bulow J.I., J.D. Geanakoplos, and P.D. Klemperer (1985), "Multimarket oligopoly: Strategic substitutes and complements," *Journal of Political Economy,* 93(3):488–511.

Calabresi G. (1968), "Transaction costs, resource allocation, and liability rules: A comment," *Journal of Law and Economics,* 11(1):67–73.

Carlin W. and C. Mayer (2003), "Finance, investment, and growth," *Journal of Financial Economics,* 69(1):191–226.

Carlsson F., J. Garcia, and A. Lofgren (2010), "Conformity and the demand for environmental goods," *Environmental and Resource Economics,* 47:407–421.

Carlsson F., O. Johansson-Stenman, and P. Martinsson (2007), "Do you enjoy having more than others? Survey evidence of positional goods," *Economica,* 74:586–598.

Chemin M. (2009a), "Do judiciaries matter for development? Evidence from India," *Journal of Comparative Economics,* 37:230–250.

Chemin M. (2009b), "The impact of the judiciary on entrepreneurship: Evaluation of Pakistan's 'Access to Justice Programme'," *Journal of Public Economics,* 93:114–125.

Chemin M. (2012), "Does court speed shape economic activity? Evidence from a court reform in India," *Journal of Law, Economics, & Organization,* 28(3):460–485.

Ciepley D. (2013), "Beyond public and private: Toward a political theory of the corporation," *American Political Science Review,* 107(1):139–158.

Clark A.E., P. Frijters, and M.A. Shields (2008), "Relative income, happiness, and utility: An explanation for the Easterlin paradox and other puzzles," *Journal of Economic Literature,* 74(2):425–467.

Clark J.M. (1926), *Social control of business*, Chicago: University of Chicago Press.

Coase R.H. (1937), "The nature of the firm," *Economica*, 4:386–406.

Coase R.H. (1959), "The federal communications commission," *Journal of Law and Economics*, 2(1):1–40.

Coase R.H. (1960), "The problem of social cost," *Journal of Law and Economics*, 3:1–44.

Coase R.H. (1972), "Industrial organization: A proposal for research," in Fuchs V. (ed.), *Policy issues and research opportunities in industrial organization*, New York: National Bureau of Economic Research, pp. 59–73.

Coase R.H. (1988), *The firm, the market and the law*, Chicago: University of Chicago Press.

Coase R.H. (1992), "The institutional structure of production," *American Economic Review*, 82(4):713–719.

Coase R.H. (2000), "The acquisition of Fisher Body by General Motors," *Journal of Law and Economics*, 43(1):15–31.

Coase R.H. (2006), "The conduct of economics: The example of Fisher Body and General Motors," *Journal of Economics & Management Strategy*, 12:255–278.

Commons J.R. (1924), *Legal foundations of capitalism*, Clifton: Augustus M. Kelley Publishers, [reprinted, 2007].

Commons J.R. (1931), "Institutional economics," *American Economic Review*, 21:648–657.

Commons J.R. (1932), "The problem of correlating law, economics and ethics," *Wisconsin Law Review*, 8:3–26.

Commons J.R. (1934), *Institutional economics*, Madison: University of Wisconsin Press, [reprinted, 1961].

Commons J.R. (1950), *The economics of collective action*, New York: Macmillan.

Commons J.R. (1959), *Institutional economics: Its place in political economy*, New York: MacMillan.

Cooter R. (1987), "Coase theorem," in Eatwell J., M. Milgate, and P. Newman (eds.), *The new Palgrave: A dictionary of economics*, vol. 1, pp. 457–460, New York: Palgrave Macmillan.

Crocker K.J. and S.E. Masten (1996), "Regulation and administered contracts revisited: Lesson from transaction-cost economics for public utility regulation," *Journal of Regulatory Economics*, 9:5–25.

Culpepper P.D. (2011), *Quiet politics and business power: Corporate control in Europe and Japan*, Cambridge: Cambridge University Press.

Dahlman C.J. (1979), "The problem of externality," *Journal of Law and Economics*, 22(1):141–162.

Deakin S., D. Gindis, G.M. Hodgson, K. Huang, and K. Pistor (2017), "Legal institutionalism: Capitalism and the constitutive role of law," *Journal of Comparative Economics*, 45:188–200.

Demsetz H. (1967), "Toward a theory of property rights," *American Economic Review*, 57(2):347–359.

Demsetz H. (1982), *Economic, legal, and political dimensions of competition*, Amsterdam: North-Holland.

Demsetz H. (1993), "The theory of the firm revisited," in Williamson O.E. and S.G. Winter (eds.), *The nature of the firm*, Oxford: Oxford University Press, pp. 159–178.

Dewey J. and A.F. Bentley (1949), *Knowing and the known*, Boston: Beacon Press. Reprinted (1973) in Handy R. and E.C. Harwood (eds.), *Useful procedures of inquiry*, Great Barrington, MA: American Institute for Economic Research, Behavioral Research Council, pp. 97–209.

DiMaggio P.J. and W.W. Powell (1991), "Introduction," in Powell W.W. and P.J. DiMaggio (eds.), *The new institutionalism in organizational science*, Chicago: University of Chicago Press, pp. 1–40.

Dixit A.K. (1980), "The role of investment in entry-deterrence," *Economic Journal*, 90:95–106.

Dixit A.K. (1996), *The making of economic policy: A transaction-cost politics perspective*, Cambridge, CA: MIT Press.

Dixit A.K. (2004), *Lawlessness and economics: Alternative modes of governance*, Princeton: Princeton University Press.

Dodd M. Jr. (1932), "For whom are corporate managers trustees?" *Harvard Law Review*, 45(8):1145–1163.

Duesenberry J.S. (1949), *Income, saving and the theory of consumer behaviour*, Harvard: University of Harvard Press.

Duxbury N. (1990), "Robert Lee Hale and the economy of legal force," *Modern Law Review*, 53(4):421–444.

Easterlin R.A. (1974), "Does economic growth improve the human lot? Some empirical evidence," in David P.A. and M.W. Reder (eds.), *Nations and households in economic growth*, New York: Academic Press, pp. 89–125.

Felice F. and M. Vatiero (2014), "Ordo and European competition law," *Research in the History of Economic Thought and Methodology*, 32:147–157.

Fiorito L. (2010), "John R. Commons, Wesley N. Hohfeld, and the origins of transactional economics," *History of Political Economy*, 42(2):267–295.

Fiorito L. and M. Vatiero (2011), "Beyond legal relations: Wesley Newcomb Hohfeld's influence on American institutionalism," *Journal of Economic Issues*, 45(1):199–222.

Frank R.H. (1985), "The demand for unobservable and other nonpositional goods," *American Economic Review*, 75(1):101–116.

Franks J. and C. Mayer (1995), "Ownership and control," in Siebert H. (ed.), *Trends in business organization: Do participation and cooperation increase competitiveness?*, Tubingen: J.C.B. Mohr, pp. 174–188.

Franks J., C. Mayer, and S. Rossi (2009), "Ownership: Evolution and regulation," *Review of Financial Studies*, 22(10):4009–4056.

Freeland R.F. (2000), "Creating holdup through vertical integration: Fisher Body revisited," *Journal of Law and Economics*, 43:32–65.

Fried B. (1998), *The progressive assault on the laissez faire: Robert Hale and the first law and economics movement*, Cambridge: Harvard University Press.

Fuller L.L. (1954), "Some reflection on legal and economic freedoms: A review of Robert L. Hale's freedom through law," *Columbia Law Review*, 54(1):70–82.

Gelter M. (2009), "The dark side of shareholder influence: Managerial autonomy and stakeholder orientation in comparative corporate governance," *Harvard International Law Journal*, 50:129–194.

Gerber D.J. (1998), *Law and competition in twentieth century Europe*, Oxford: Oxford University Press.

Gibbons R. (2005), "Four formal(izable) theories of the firm?," *Journal of Economic Behavior and Organization*, 58:200–245.

Giocoli N. (2014), *Predatory pricing in antitrust law and economics. A historical perspective*. London: Routledge.

Giocoli N. (2017), "Love me, love me not. The complicated affair between classical economics and American corporations during the Gilded Age," work in progress, *on file with author*.

Glaeser E.L. and A. Shleifer (2002), "Legal origins," *Quarterly Journal of Economics*, 117(4):1193–1229.

Gourevitch P.A. and J.J. Shinn (2005), *Political power and corporate control: The new global politics of corporate governance*, Princeton: Princeton University Press.

Gravelle H. and R. Rees (1981), *Microeconomics*, London: Longman.

Hale R.L. (1923), "Coercion and distribution in a supposedly non-coercive state," *Political Science Quarterly*, 38(3):470–494.

Hale R.L. (1935a), "Force and state: A comparison of 'political' and 'economic' compulsion," *Columbia Law Review*, 35(2):149–201.

Hale R.L. (1935b), "Unconstitutional conditions and constitutional rights," *Columbia Law Review*, 35(3):321–359.

Hale R.L. (1939), "Our equivocal constitutional guaranties. Treacherous safeguards of liberty," *Columbia Law Review*, 39(4):563–594.

Hale R.L. (1943), "Bargaining, duress, and economic liberty," *Columbia Law Review*, 43(5):603–628.

Hale R.L. (1951), "Economic liberty and the state," *Political Science Quarterly*, 66(3):400–410.

Hale R.L. (1952), *Freedom through law: Public control of private governing power*, New York: Columbia University Press.

Hall P.A. and D. Soskice (2001), "An introduction to varieties of capitalism," in Hall P.A. and D. Soskice (eds.), *Varieties of capitalism: The institutional foundations of comparative advantage*, Oxford: Oxford University Press, pp. 1–68.

Hamilton W.H. (1932), "Institution," in Seligman E.R.A. and A. Johnson (eds.), *Encyclopaedia of the social sciences*, vol. 8, New York: Macmillan, pp. 84–89.

Hansmann H. and R. Kraakman (2001), "The end of history for corporate law," *Georgetown Law Journal*, 89:439–468.

Hart O. (1995), *Firms, contracts and financial structure*, Oxford: Oxford University Press.

Hart O. (2017), "Incomplete contracts and control," *American Economic Review*, 107(7):1731–1752.

Hodgson G.M. (1988), *Economics and institutions: A manifesto for a modern institutional economics*, Cambridge: Polity Press.

Hodgson G.M. (2006), "What are institutions?," *Journal of Economic Issues*, 40(1):1–25.

Hodgson G.M. (2015), "Much of the 'economics of property rights' devalues property and legal rights," *Journal of Institutional Economics*, 11(4):725–730.

Hohfeld W.N. (1913), "Some fundamental legal conceptions as applied in judicial reasoning," *Yale Law Journal*, 23(1):16–59.

Hohfeld W.N. (1917), "Fundamental legal conceptions as applied in judicial reasoning," *Yale Law Journal*, 26(8):710–770.

Holmes O.W. (1881), *The common law*, Boston: Little Brown.

Hopkins E. and T. Kornienko (2004), "Running to keep in the same place: Consumer choice as a game of status," *American Economic Review*, 94(4):1085–1107.

Klein B. (1996), "Why hold-ups occur: The self-enforcing range of contractual relationships," *Economic Inquiry*, 34:444–463.

Klein B. and K.M. Murphy (1997), "Vertical integration as a self-enforcing contractual arrangement," *American Economic Review*, 87(2):415–420.

Knight F.H. (1921), *Risk, uncertainty and profit*, Boston: Houghton Mifflin.

Koss P. (1999), "Self-enforcing transactions: Reciprocal exposure in fisheries," *Journal of Law and Economics*, 43:105–141.

Lamm M. (1978), "The Fisher brothers: Their lives and times," *Special Interest Autos, Hemming Motor News*, 45, May–June:n.a.

Landes W. and R. Posner (1975), "The independent judiciary in an interest-group perspective," *Journal of Law and Economics*, 18(3):875–901.

La Porta R., F. Lopez-de-Silanes, and A. Shleifer (1999), "Corporate ownership around the world," *Journal of Finance*, 54(2):471–517.

La Porta R., F. Lopez-de-Silanes, and A. Shleifer (2000), "Investor protection and corporate governance," *Journal of Financial Economics*, 57:1147–1170.

La Porta R., F. Lopez-de-Silanes, and A. Shleifer (2008), "The economic consequences of legal origins," *Journal of Economic Literature*, 46(2):285–335.

La Porta R., F. Lopez-de-Silanes, A. Shleifer, and R.W. Vishny (1997), "Legal determinants of external finance," *Journal of Finance*, 52(3):1131–1150.

La Porta R., F. Lopez-de-Silanes, A. Shleifer, and R.W. Vishny (1998), "Law and finance," *Journal of Political Economy*, 106(6):1113–1155.

Lechevalier S. (2014), *The great transformation of Japanese capitalism*, New York: Routledge.

Lele P.P. and M.M. Siems (2007), "Shareholder protection: A leximetric approach," *Journal of Corporate Law Studies*, 7:17–50.

Luttmer E.F.P. (2005), "Neighbors as negatives: Relative earnings and well-being," *Quarterly Journal of Economics*, 120(3):963–1002.

Macneil I.R. (1978), "Contracts: Adjustment of long-term economic relations under classical, neoclassical, and relational contract law," *Northwestern University Law Review*, 72(4):854–905.

March J.G. (1962), "The business firm as a political coalition," *Journal of Politics*, 24(4):662–678.

Marglin S. (1974), "What do bosses do?," *Review of Radical Political Economy*, 6:33–60.

Matthews R.C.O. (1986), "The economics of institutions and the sources of growth," *Economic Journal*, 96:903–918.

Mayer C. (2000), *Ownership matters*, inaugural lecture, Brussels: Université Libre de Bruxelles.

McAdams R.H. (1992), "Relative preferences," *Yale Law Journal*, 102(1):1–104.

Medema S.G. (2009), *The hesitant hand. Taming self-interest in the history of economic ideas*, Princeton: Princeton University Press.

Medema S.G. (2017), "The Coase Theorem at sixty," work in progress, *on file with author*.

Mercuro N., S.G. Medema, and W.J. Samuels (2006), "Robert Lee Hale (1884–1969): Legal economist," in Backhaus J.G. (ed.), *The Elgar companion to law and economics*, Cheltenham: Edward Elgar, pp. 531–544.

Merrill T. and H.E. Smith (2001a), "What happened to property in law and economics?," *Yale Law Journal*, 111:357–398.

Merrill T. and H.E. Smith (2001b), "The property/contract interface," *Columbia Law Review*, 110:773–852.

Milgrom P. and J. Roberts (1990), "Rationability, learning and equilibrium in games with strategic complementarities," *Econometrica*, 58:1255–1277.

Mill J.S. (1859), *On liberty*, London: Longman, Roberts, & Green Co.

Morck R.K., D. Wolfenzon, and B. Yeung (2005), "Corporate governance, economic entrenchment, and growth," *Journal of Economic Literature*, 43:655–720.

Neumark D. and A. Postlewaite (1993), "Relative income concerns and the rise in married women's employment," *Journal of Public Economics*, 70:157–183.

Nicita A. and M. Vatiero (2014), "Dixit versus Williamson: The 'fundamental transformation' reconsidered," *European Journal of Law and Economics*, 37(3):439–453.

Nicoletti G., S. Scarpetta, and O. Boylaud (2000), *Summary indicators of product market regulation with an extension to employment protection legislation*, Paris: OECD Economics Department Working Papers No. 226.

North D.C. (1990a), *Institutions, institutional change, and economic performance*, Cambridge: Cambridge University Press.

North D.C. (1990b), "A transaction cost theory of politics," *Journal of Theoretical Politics*, 2(4):355–367.

North D.C. (1995), "Five propositions about institutional change," in Knight J. and I. Sened (eds.), *Explaining social institutions*, Michigan: Michigan University Press, pp. 15–26.

Olson M. (1965), *The logic of collective action*, Cambridge, MA: Harvard University Press.

Olson M. (1982), *The rise and decline of nations: Economic growth, stagflation, and social rigidities*, New Haven: Yale University Press.

Pagano M. and P.F. Volpin (2005), "The political economy of corporate governance," *American Economic Review*, 95(4):1005–1030.

Pagano U. (1999), "Is power an economic good? Notes on social scarcity and the economics of positional goods," in Bowles S., M. Franzini, and U. Pagano (eds.), *The politics and the economics of power*, London: Routledge, pp. 116–145.

Pagano U. (2012a), "No institution is a free lunch: A reconstruction of Ronald Coase," *International Review of Economics*, 59(2):189–200.

Pagano U. (2012b), "The evolution of the American corporation and global organizational biodiversity," *Seattle University Law Review*, 35(4):1271–1298.

Pagano U. (2019), "Economic things, legal persons and the hybrid business corporation," work in progress, *on file with author*.

Pagano U. and M. Vatiero (2015), "Costly institutions as substitutes: Novelty and limits of the Coasian approach," *Journal of Institutional Economics*, 11(2: Coase memorial issue):265–281.

Pagano U. and M. Vatiero (2019), "Positional goods and legal orderings," in Marciano A. and G.B. Ramello (eds.), *Encyclopaedia of Law and Economics*, Berlin: Springer.

Perotti E.C. and E.L. von Thadden (2006), "The political economy of corporate control and labor rents," *Journal of Political Economy*, 114(1):145–175.

Pistor K. (2019), *The code of capital: How the law creates wealth and inequality*, Princeton: Princeton University Press.

Polanyi K. (1968), *Primitive, archaic and modern economies: Essays of Karl Polanyi*, New York: Doubleday/Anchor Books.

Ponticelli J. and L.S. Alencar (2016), "Court enforcement, bank loans and firm investment: Evidence from a bankruptcy reform in Brazil," *Quarterly Journal of Economics*, 131:1365–1413.

Rajan R.R. and L. Zingales (1998), "Power in a theory of the firm," *Quarterly Journal of Economics*, 113(1):387–432.

Rajan R.R. and L. Zingales (2003), "The great reversals: The politics of financial development in the twentieth century," *Journal of Financial Economics*, 69:5–50.

Raub W. and G. Keren (1993), "Hostages as a commitment device: A game-theoretic model and an empirical test of some scenarios," *Journal of Economic Behavior and Organization*, 21:43–67.

Roe M.J. (1994), *Strong managers, weak owners: The political roots of American corporate finance*, Princeton: Princeton University Press.

Roe M.J. (2002), "Corporate law's limits," *Journal of Legal Studies*, 31(2):233–271.

Roe M.J. (2003), *Political determinants of corporate governance: Political context, corporate impact*, Oxford: Oxford University Press.

Roe M.J. (2006), "Legal origins, politics and modern stock markets," *Harvard Law Review*, 120(2):462–527.

Roe M.J. (2019), "Stock market short-termism's impact," *University of Pennsylvania Law Review*, 167:71–121.

Roe M.J. and M. Vatiero (2018), "Corporate governance and its political economy," in Gordon J.N. and W.-G. Ringe (eds.), *Oxford handbook of corporate law and governance*, Oxford: Oxford University Press, pp. 56–83.

Rose N.L. (1987), "Labor rent sharing and regulation: Evidence from the trucking industry," *Journal of Political Economy*, 95(6):1146–1178.

Rutherford M. (2001), "Institutional economics: Then and now," *Journal of Economic Perspectives*, 15(3):173–194.

Salinger M.A. (1984), "Tobin's q, unionization, and the concentration-profits relationship," *RAND Journal of Economics*, 15(2):159–170.

Samuels W.J. (1973), "The economy as a system of power and its legal bases: The legal economics of Robert Lee Hale," *University of Miami Law Review*, 27(3):261–371.

Samuelson P.A. (1947), "Foundations of economic analysis," in *Harvard Economic Studies*, vol. 80, Cambridge: Harvard University Press.

Samuelson P.A. (1954), "The pure theory of public expenditure," *Review of Economics and Statistics*, 36:387–389.

Samuelson P.A. (1955), "Diagrammatic exposition of a theory of public expenditure," *Review of Economics and Statistics*, 37(4):350–356.

Samuelson P.A. (1974), "Complementarity: An essay on the 40th anniversary of the Hicks-Allen revolution in demand theory," *Journal of Economic Literature*, 12(4):1255–1289.

Schelling T. (1960), *The strategy of conflict*, Oxford: Oxford University Press.

Sen A.K. (1983), "Poor, relatively speaking," *Oxford Economic Papers*, 35:153–169.

Shavell S. (2009), "Why breach of contract may not be immoral given the incompleteness of contracts," *Michigan Law Review*, 107:1569–1581.

Siems M.M. (2007), "Legal origins: Reconciling law and finance and comparative law," *McGill Law Journal*, 52:55–81.

Smith A. (1762–1766), *Lectures on jurisprudence* [printed 1978] Meek R.L., D.D. Raphael and P.G. Stein (eds.), Oxford: Clarendon Press.

Smith H.E. (2017), "Property as complex interaction," *Journal of Institutional Economics*, 13(4):809–814.

Solnick S.J. and D. Hemenway (1998), "Is more always better? A survey on positional concerns," *Journal of Economic Behavior and Organization*, 37(3):373–383.

Solnick S.J. and D. Hemenway (2005), "Are positional concerns stronger in some domains than in others?," *American Economic Review*, 95(2):147–151.

Spamann H. (2010), "The 'Antidirector rights index' revisited," *Review of Financial Studies*, 23(2):467–486.

Spence M. (1977), "Entry, capacity, investment and oligopolistic pricing," *Bell Journal of Economics*, 8(2):534–544.

Spiller T.P. (2013), "Transaction cost regulation," *Journal of Economic Behavior and Organization*, 89:232–242.

Stigler G.J. (1966), *The theory of price*, New York: MacMillan.

Stigler G.J. (1971), "The theory of economic regulation," *Bell Journal of Economics and Management Science*, 2(1):3–21.

Streeck W. (2011), *Re-forming capitalism: Institutional change in the German political economy*, Oxford: Oxford University Press.

Sunstein C.R. and E. Ullman-Margalit (2001), "Solidarity goods," *Journal of Political Philosophy*, 9(2):129–149.

Sylos-Labini P. (1969), *Oligopoly and technical progress*, Cambridge: Harvard University Press.

Tirole J. (1999), "Incomplete contracts: Where do we stand?," *Econometrica*, 67(4):741–781.

Tirole J. (2006), *The theory of corporate finance*, Princeton: Princeton University Press.

Tullock G. (1980), "Two kinds of legal efficiency," *Hofstra Law Review*, 8(3):659–670.

Vatiero M. (2010a), "The ordoliberal notion of market power: An institutionalist reassessment," *European Competition Journal*, 6:689–707.

Vatiero M. (2010b), "From W.N. Hohfeld to J.R. Commons, and beyond? Enquiry on jural relations," *American Journal of Economics and Sociology*, 69(2):840–866.

Vatiero M. (2013), "Positional goods and Robert Lee Hale's legal economics," *Journal of Institutional Economics*, 9(3):351–362.

Vatiero M. (2015), "Dominant market position and ordoliberalism," *International Review of Economics*, 62(4):291–306.

Vatiero M. (2017a), "On the (political) origin of 'corporate governance' species," *Journal of Economic Surveys*, 31(2):393–409.

Vatiero M. (2017b), "Learning from Swiss corporate governance exception," *Kyklos*, 70(2):330–343.

Vatiero M. (2018), "Transaction and transactors' choices: What we have learned and what we need to explore," in Ménard C. and M.M. Shirley (eds.), *A research agenda for New Institutional Economics*, Cheltenham: Edward Elgar Publishing, pp. 97–107.

Veblen T. (1899), *The theory of the leisure class: An economic study in the evolution of institutions*, New York: MacMillan.

Veblen T. (1914), The instinct of workmanship and the state of the industrial arts, New York: MacMillan.

Veblen T. (1923), *Absentee ownership and business enterprise in recent times: The case of America*, New York: Viking Press.

Veljanovski C.G. (1982), "The Coase theorems and the economic theory of markets and law," *Kyklos*, 35(1):53–74.

Visaria S. (2009), "Legal reform and loan repayment: The microeconomic impact of debt recovery tribunals in India," *American Economic Journal: Applied Economics*, 3:59–81.

Weingast B.R. (1995), "The economic role of political institutions: Market-preserving federalism and economic development," *Journal of Law, Economics, & Organization*, 11(1):1–31.

Williamson O.E. (1973), "Markets and hierarchies: Some elementary considerations," *American Economic Review*, 63(2):316–325.

Williamson O.E. (1975), *Markets and hierarchies: Analysis and antitrust implications*, New York: Free Press.

Williamson O.E. (1979), "Transaction-cost economics: The governance of contractual relations," *Journal of Law and Economics*, 22(2):233–261.

Williamson O.E. (1981), "The economics of organization: The transaction cost approach," *American Journal of Sociology*, 87(3):548–577.

Williamson O.E. (1983), "Credible commitments: Using hostages to support exchange," *American Economic Review*, 73(4):519–540.

Williamson O.E. (1985a), *The economic institutions of capitalism*, New York: Free Press.

Williamson O.E. (1985b), "Assessing contracts," *Journal of Law, Economics, & Organization*, 1:177–208.

Williamson O.E. (1988), "Corporate finance and corporate governance," *Journal of Finance*, 43(3):567–591.

Williamson O.E. (1989), "Transaction cost economics," in Schmalensee R. and R. Willig (eds.), *Handbook of industrial organization*, vol. 1, North Holland: Elsevier, pp. 136–182.

Williamson O.E. (1990a), "Chester Barnard and the incipient science of organization," in Williamson O.E. (ed.), *Organization theory: From Chester Barnard to the present and beyond*, Oxford: Oxford University Press, pp. 172–206.

Williamson O.E. (1990b), "The firm as a nexus of treaties: An introduction," in Aoki M., B. Gustafsson, and O.E. Williamson (eds.), *The firm as a nexus of treaties*, London: Sage Publications, pp. 1–25.

Williamson O.E. (1993), "Introduction," in Williamson O.E. and S.G. Winter (eds.), *The nature of the firm*, Oxford: Oxford University Press, pp. 3–17.

Williamson O.E. (1996a), "Prologue: The mechanisms of governance," in Williamson O.E. (ed.), *The mechanism of governance*, Oxford: Oxford University Press.

Williamson O.E. (1996b), "Economic organization: The case for candor," *Academy of Management Review*, 21(1):48–57.

Williamson O.E. (1996c), "Transaction cost economics and the Carnegie connection," *Journal of Economic Behavior and Organization*, 31(2):149–155.

Williamson O.E. (1999), *Human actors and economic organization*, Quaderni del dipartimento di economia politica, no. 247, Siena: Università degli Studi di Siena.

Williamson O.E. (2000), "The new institutional economics: Taking stock, looking ahead," *Journal of Economic Literature*, 38:595–613.

Williamson O.E. (2002), "The theory of the firm as governance structure: From choice to contract," *Journal of Economic Perspectives*, 16(3):171–195.

Williamson O.E. (2005), "The economics of governance," *American Economic Review*, 95(2):1–18.

Williamson O.E. (2010), "Transaction cost economics: An overview," in Klein P.G. and M.E. Sykuta (eds.), *The Elgar companion to transaction cost economics*, Aldershot: Edward Elgar, pp. 8–26.

Zingales L. (2017), "Towards a political theory of the firm," *Journal of Economic Perspectives*, 31(3):113–130.

Index

Note: Page numbers in *italics* indicate figures and page numbers in **bold** indicate tables on the corresponding pages.

Printed in the United States
by Baker & Taylor Publisher Services